HAL•LEONARD®

GUITAR PLAY-ALONG

VOL. 74

SIMPLE STRUMMING SONGS

AUDIO ACCESS INCLUDED

PLAYBACK+
Speed • Pitch • Balance • Loop

CONTENTS

2 American Pie
DON McCLEAN

17 Baby, I Love Your Way
PETER FRAMPTON

24 Barely Breathing
DUNCAN SHEIK

34 Boulevard of Broken Dreams
GREEN DAY

40 Chasing Cars
SNOW PATROL

46 Drops of Jupiter (Tell Me)
TRAIN

64 Half of My Heart
JOHN MAYER

57 Hey Jude
THE BEATLES

72 A Horse with No Name
AMERICA

80 Island in the Sun
WEEZER

85 One
U2

122 Redemption Song
BOB MARLEY

94 The Scientist
COLDPLAY

102 Sunny Came Home
SHAWN COLVIN

112 What's Up
4 NON BLONDES

T0116614

To access audio visit:
www.halleonard.com/mylibrary

Enter Code
8213-0331-0772-4455

ISBN 978-1-4950-4735-0

HAL•LEONARD®
7777 W. BLUEMOUND RD. P.O. BOX 13819 MILWAUKEE, WI 53213

For all works contained herein:
Unauthorized copying, arranging, adapting, recording, Internet posting, public performance, or other distribution of the printed or recorded music in this publication is an infringement of copyright.
Infringers are liable under the law.

Visit Hal Leonard Online at
www.halleonard.com

American Pie

Words and Music by Don McLean

Copyright © 1971, 1972 BENNY BIRD CO., INC.
Copyright Renewed
All Rights Controlled and Administered by SONGS OF UNIVERSAL, INC.
All Rights Reserved Used by Permission

Em Am Em Am
But Feb - ru - ar - y made me shiv - er, with ev - 'ry pa - per I'd de - liv - er.
C G/B Am C D G D/F♯ Em
Bad news on the door - step; I could-n't take one more step. I can't re-mem - ber if I cried when I
C D G D/F♯ Em
read a - bout his wid-owed bride. But some-thing touched me deep in - side,
C D G
the day the mu - sic died. So

Chorus
Moderately ♩= 101
G C G D G C
bye, bye, Miss A - mer - i - can Pie. Drove my Chev - y to the lev - ee, but the
G D G C G D
lev - ee was dry. An' them good ol' boys were drink - in' whis-key an' rye, sing - in',
Em A7 Em
"This - 'll be the day that I die, this - 'll be the day that I
Faster ♩= 141
D7 D7sus2 D7 D7sus4 D7 D7sus2 D7
die."

Verse
G
Am
C
1. Did you write the book of love and do you have faith in
2. See additional lyrics
Am
Em
D7
D7sus2
D7
God a - bove, if the Bi - ble tells you so?
D7sus4
D7
D7sus2
D7
G
D/F♯
Em
Now do you be - lieve in rock 'n' roll? Can
Am7
C
Em
mu - sic save your mor - tal soul? An' can you teach me

A7 A7sus2 A7 D7 D7sus2 D7 D7sus4 D7
how to dance real slow? Well, I
Em D7 Em
know that you're in love with him, 'cause I saw you danc - in'
D7 C G Am Asus2 Am
in the gym. You both kicked off your shoes. Man, I
C D7 G D/F♯
dig those Rhy-thm and Blues. I was a lone - ly teen - age

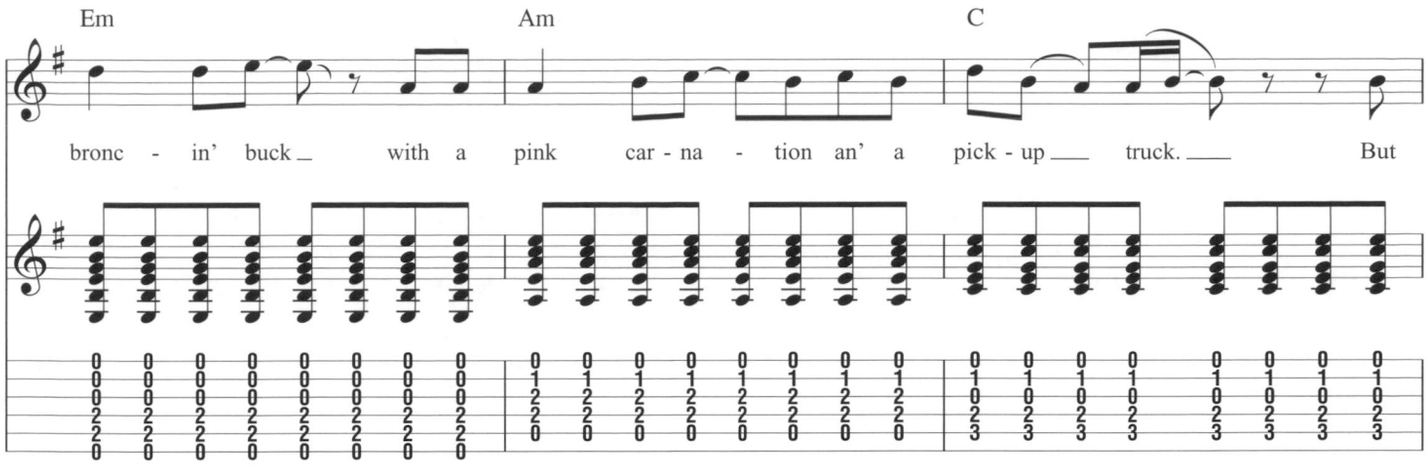
Em Am C
bronc - in' buck with a pink car - na - tion an' a pick - up truck. But

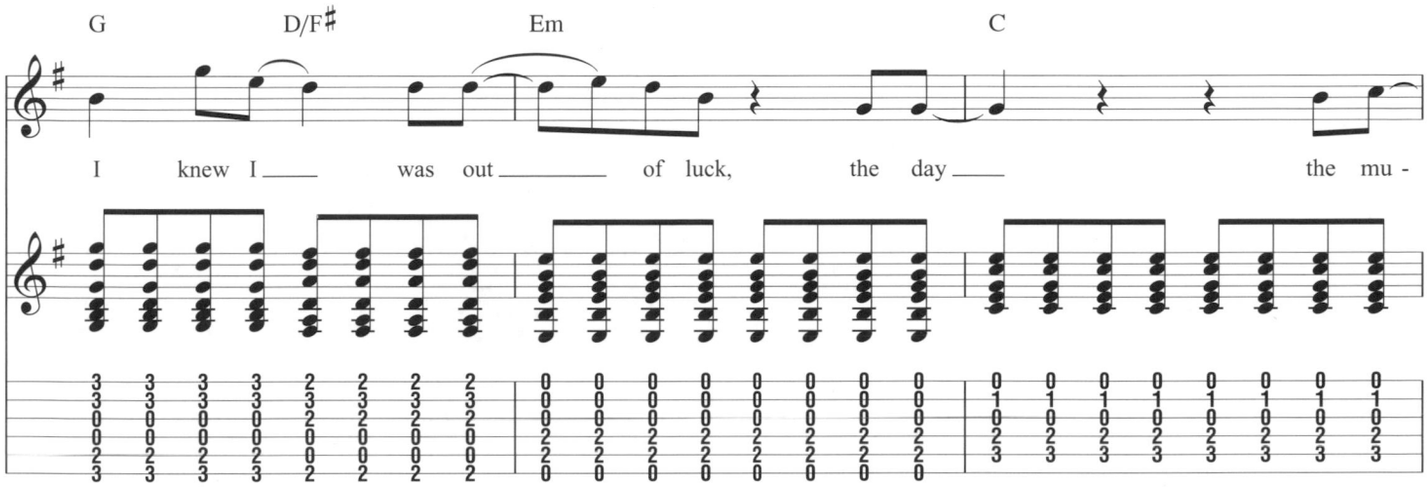
G D/F♯ Em C
I knew I was out of luck, the day the mu -

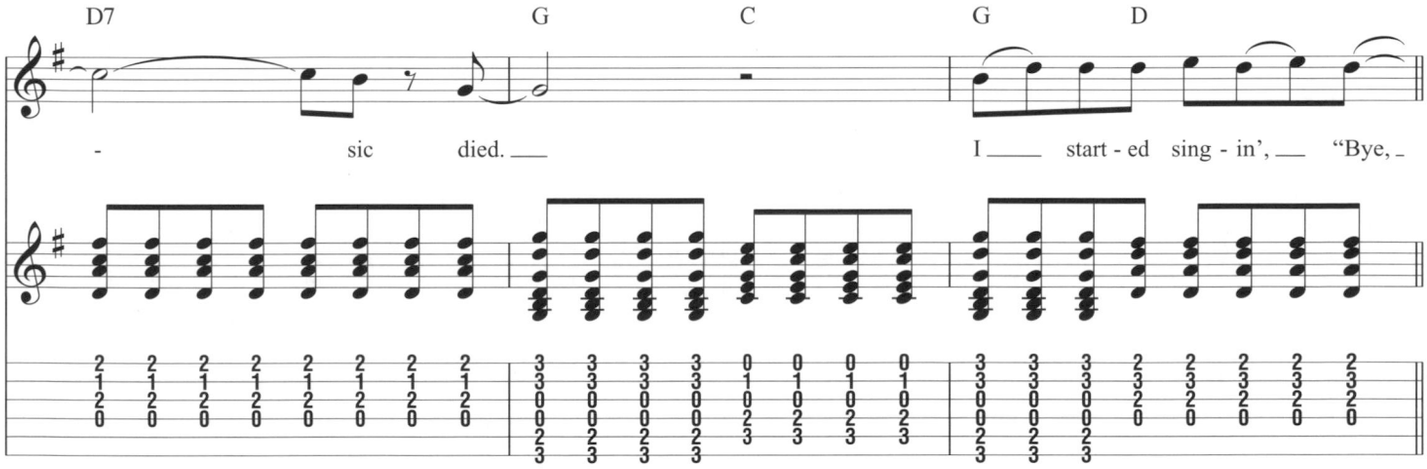
D7 G C G D
- sic died. I start - ed sing - in', "Bye,

Chorus

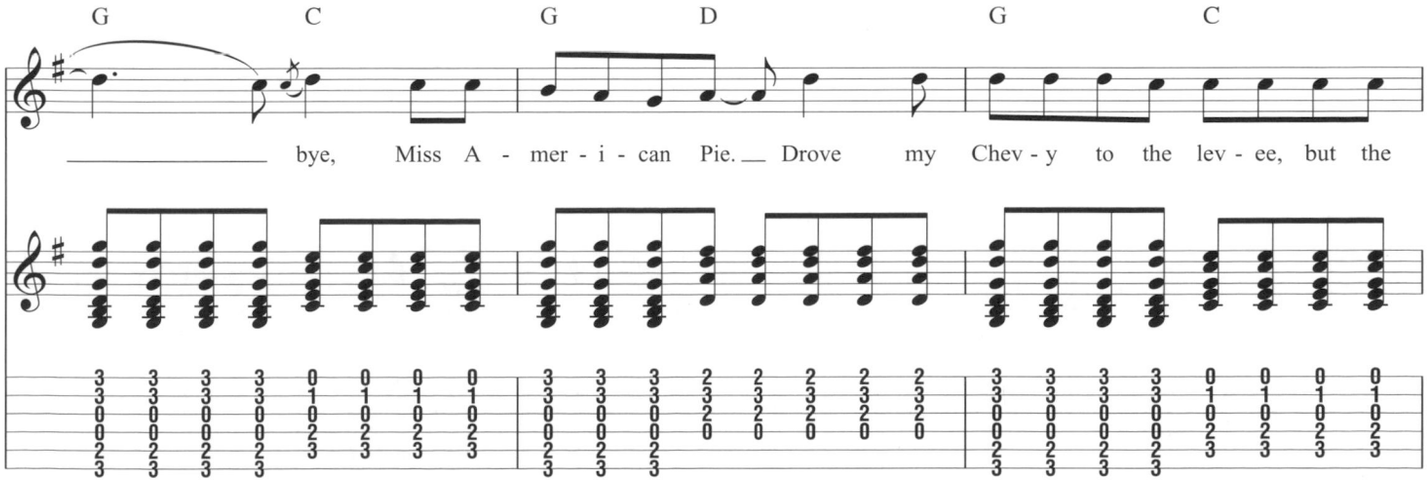
G C G D G C
bye, Miss A - mer - i - can Pie. Drove my Chev - y to the lev - ee, but the

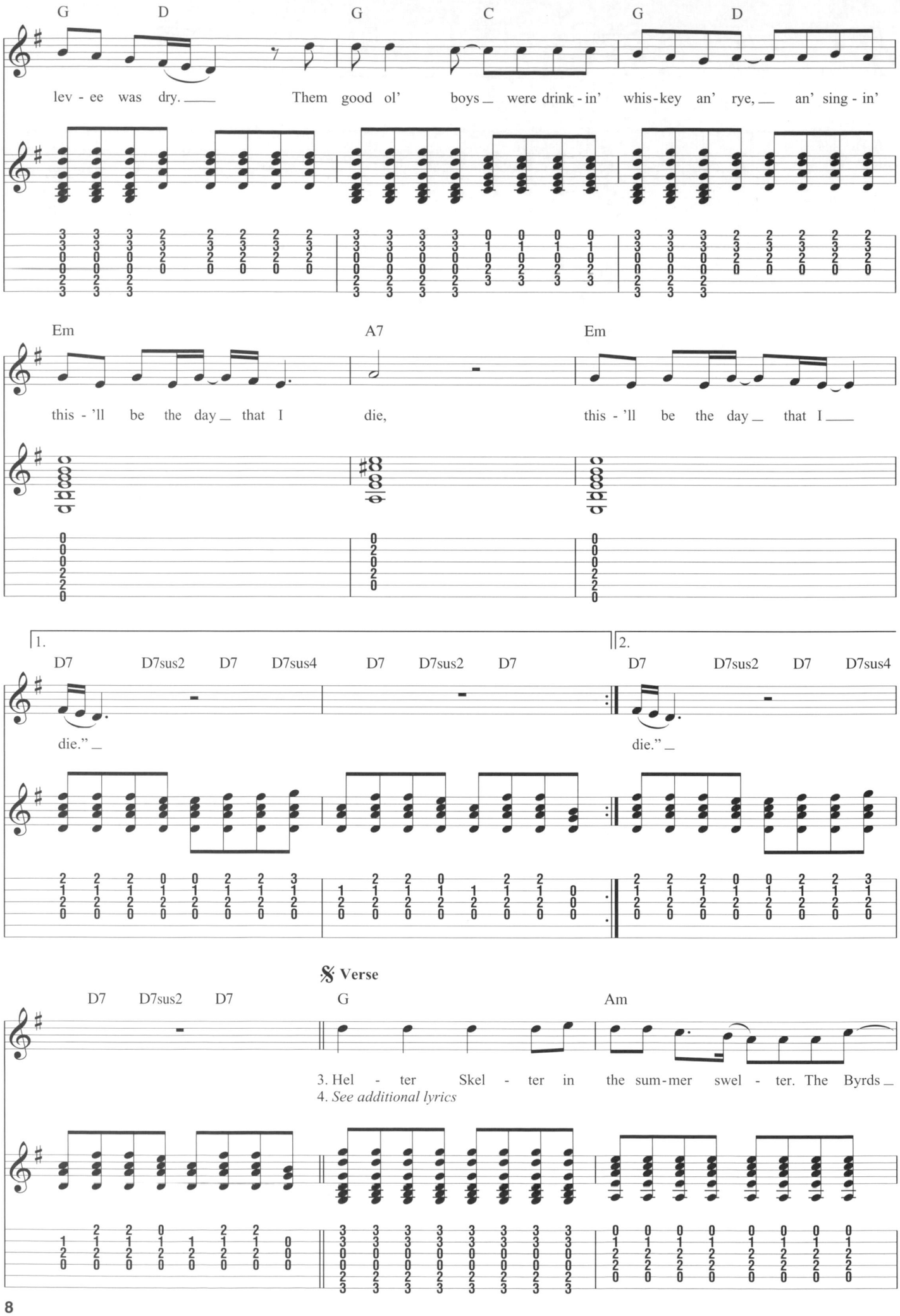
G D G C G D
lev - ee was dry. Them good ol' boys were drink - in' whis - key an' rye, an' sing - in'
Em A7 Em
this - 'll be the day that I die, this - 'll be the day that I
1.
D7 D7sus2 D7 D7sus4 D7 D7sus2 D7
die."
2.
D7 D7sus2 D7 D7sus4
die."
𝄋 Verse
D7 D7sus2 D7 G Am
3. Hel - ter Skel - ter in the sum - mer swel - ter. The Byrds
4. See additional lyrics

C Am Em
flew off with a fall - out shel - ter, eight miles high an'
D7 D7sus2 D7 D7sus4 D7 D7sus2 D7 G D/F♯
fall - in' fast. It land - ed foul out
Em Am7 C
on the grass. The play - ers tried for a for - ward pass, with the
Em A7 A7sus2 A7 D7 D7sus2 D7
jest - er on the side - lines in a cast.

D7sus4 D7
Em
D
Now, the half - time air was sweet per - fume, while
Em
D7
C
G
the ser - geants played a march - in' tune. We all got up to dance,
Am
Asus2
Am
C
D7
oh, but we nev - er got the chance. 'Cause the
G
D/F♯
Em
Am
play - ers tried to take the field, the march - ing band re -

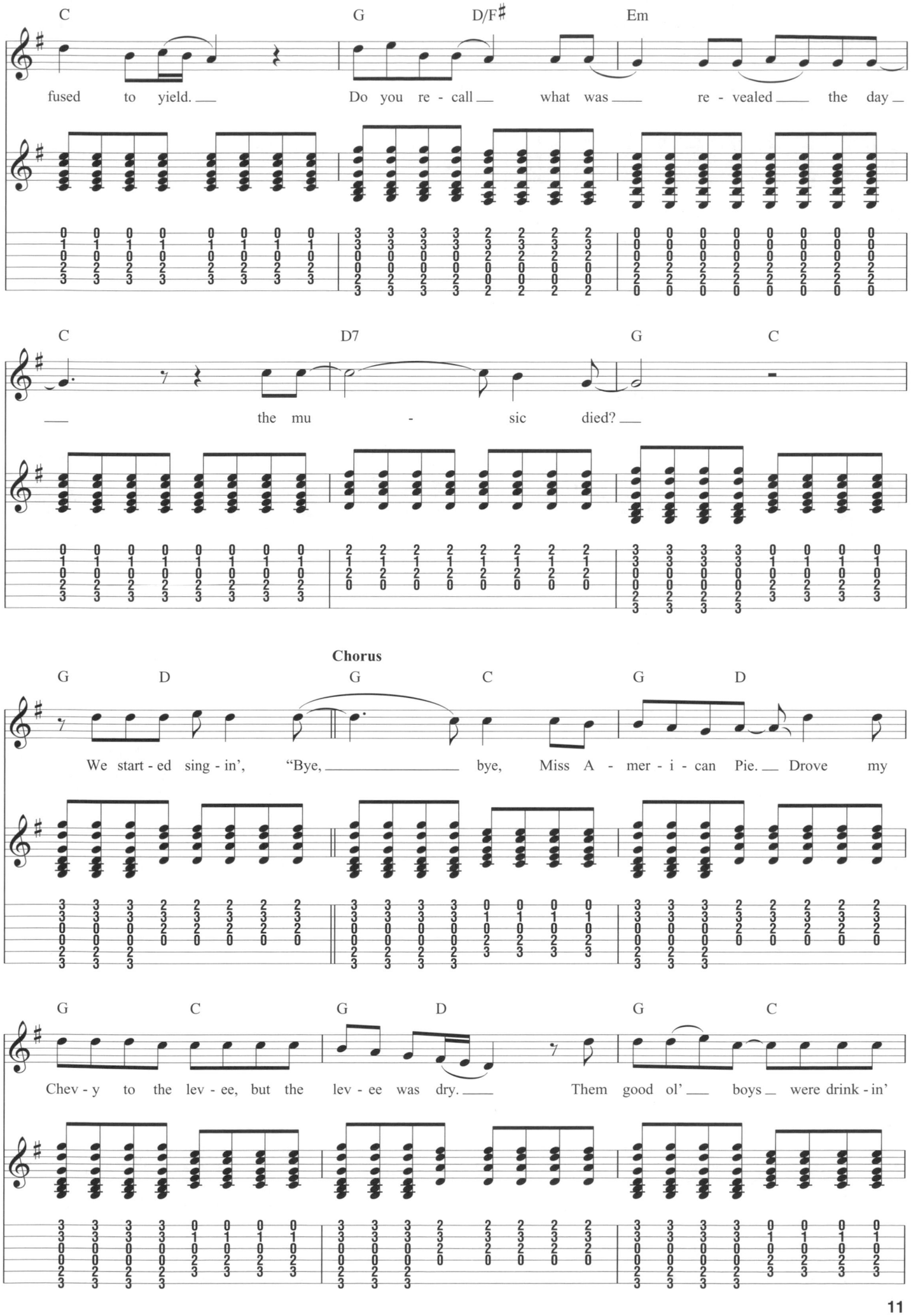
C G D/F♯ Em
fused to yield. Do you re - call what was re - vealed the day
C D7 G C
the mu - sic died?
Chorus
G D G C G D
We start - ed sing - in', "Bye, bye, Miss A - mer - i - can Pie. Drove my
G C G D G C
Chev - y to the lev - ee, but the lev - ee was dry. Them good ol' boys were drink - in'

G D Em A7
whis - key an' rye, an' sing - in' this - 'll be the day that I die,
To Coda
D.S. al Coda
Em D7 D7sus2 D7 D7sus4 D7 D7sus2 D7
this - 'll be the day that I die." 4. Oh, and
Coda
Verse
Rubato
Half-time feel
D G D/F♯ Em
die." 5. I met a girl who sang the blues and
Am C Em D
I asked her for some hap-py news. But she just smiled and turned a-way.

G D/F♯ Em Am C
I went down to the sa - cred store, where I'd heard the mu - sic years be - fore. But the
Em C D
man there said the mu - sic would-n't play. And
Em Am Em Am
in the streets the chil - dren screamed, the lov - ers cried and the po - ets dreamed. But
C G/B Am C D G D/F♯ Em
not a word was spo-ken; the church bells all were bro - ken. And the three men I ad-mire most, the

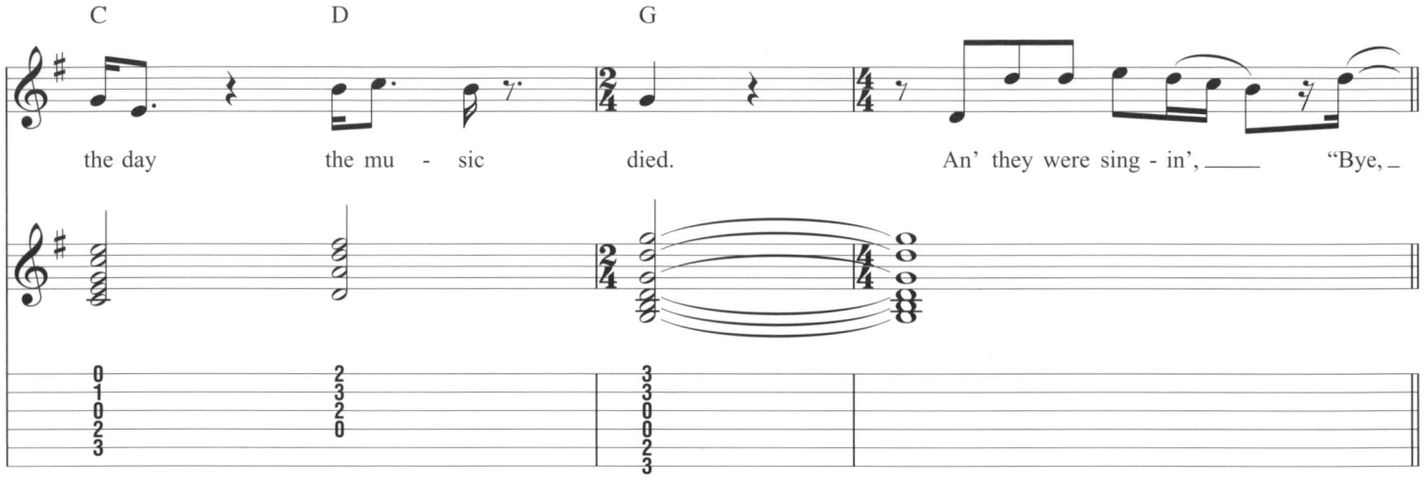

Chorus

Moderately slow ♩ = 90

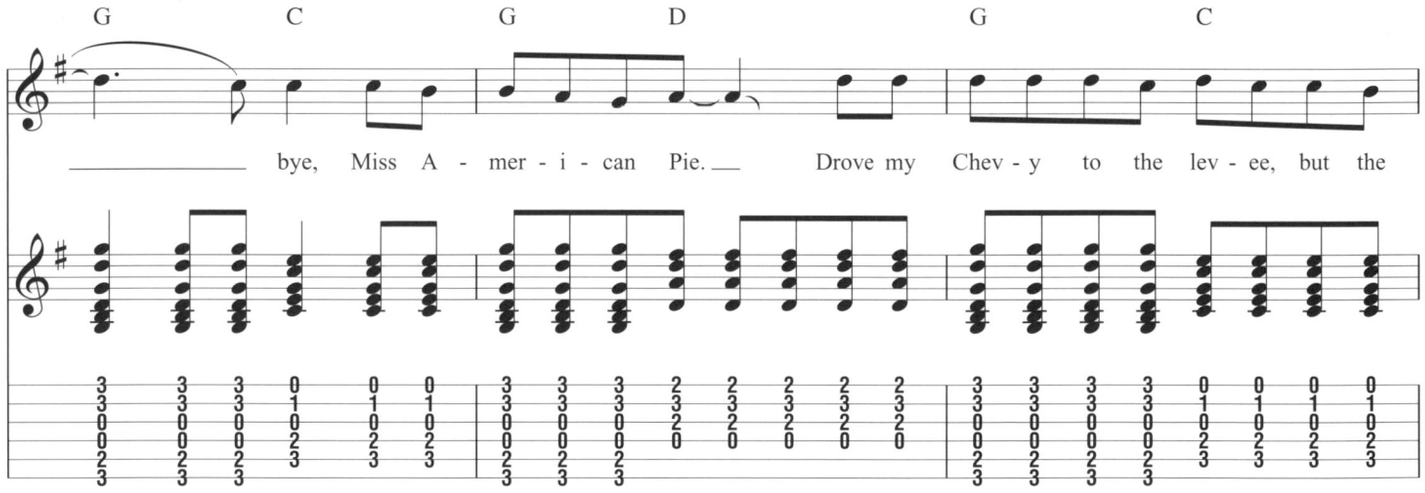

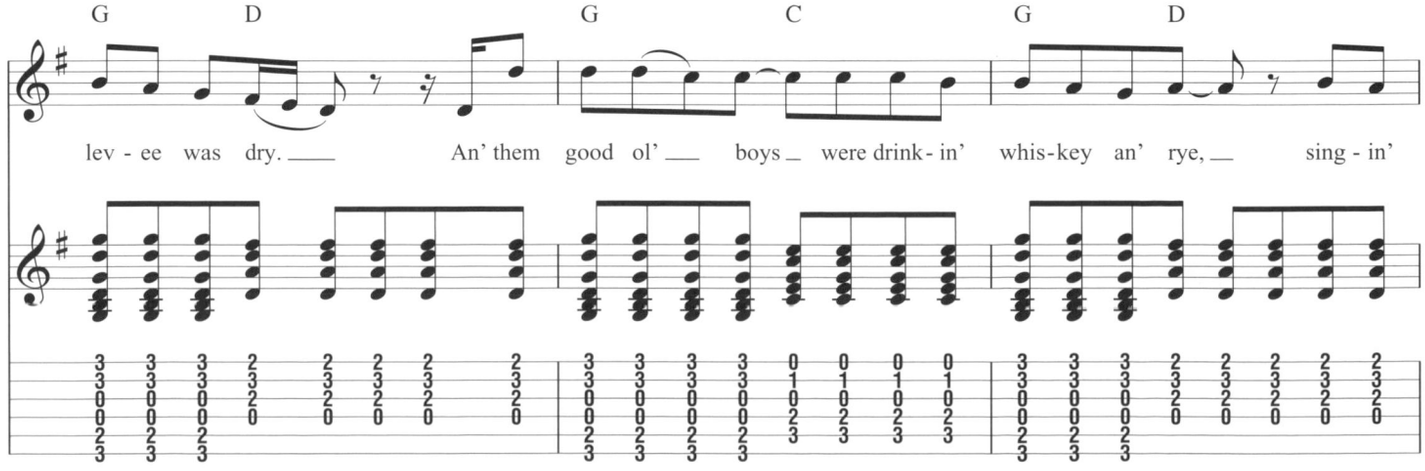

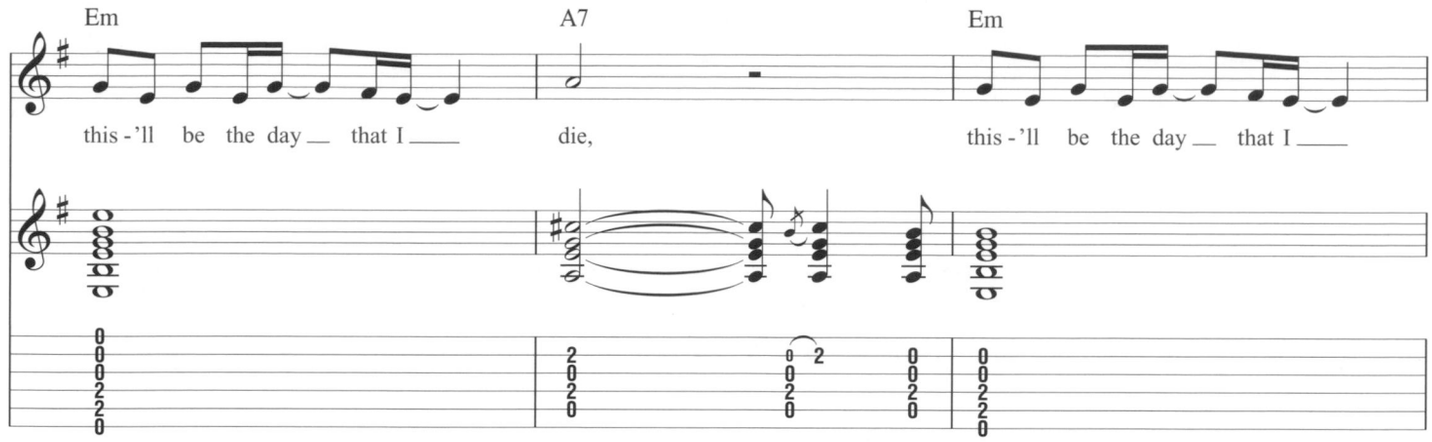

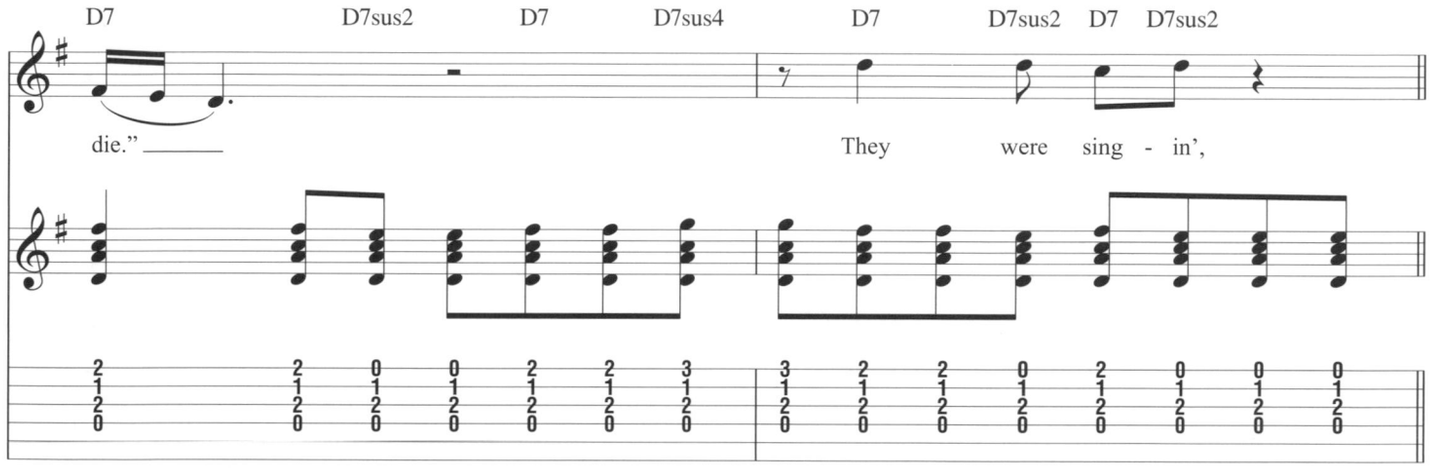

Outro-Chorus
Faster ♩ = 102

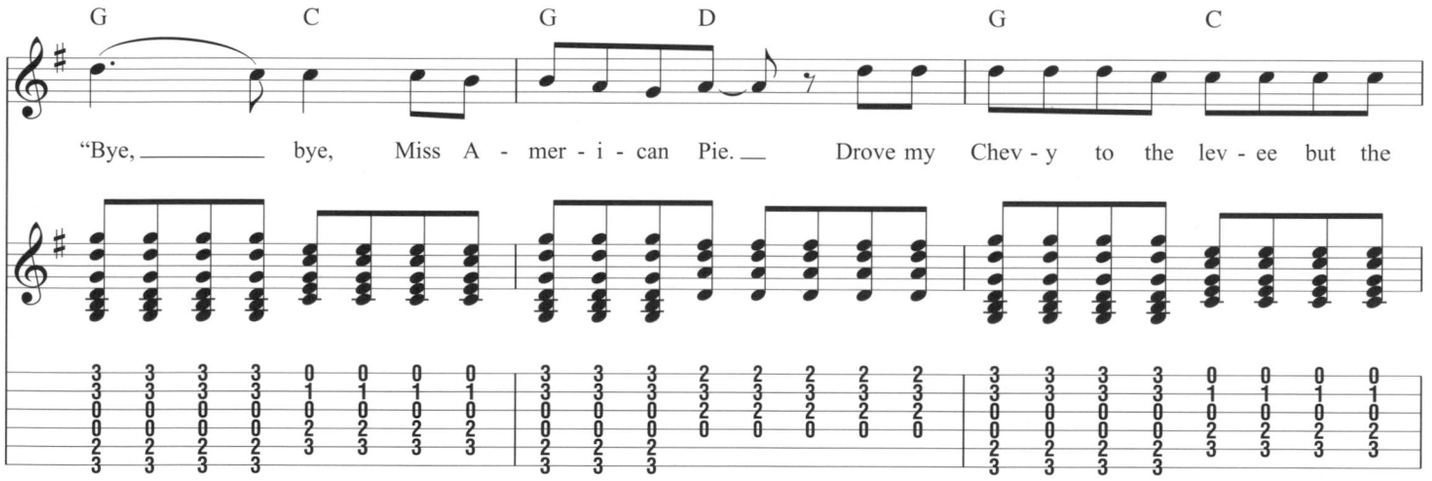

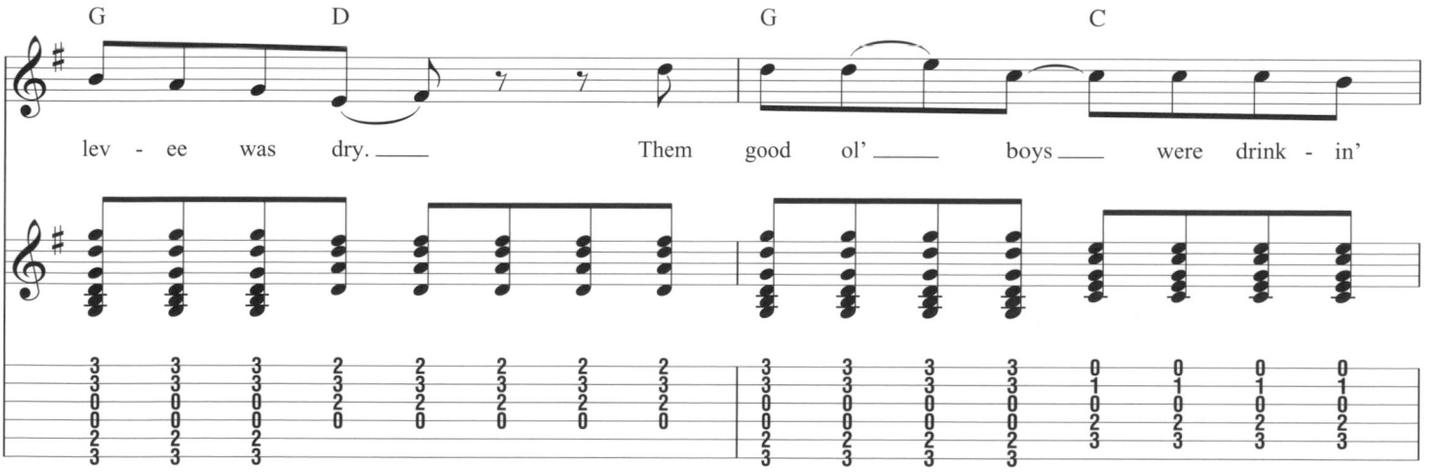

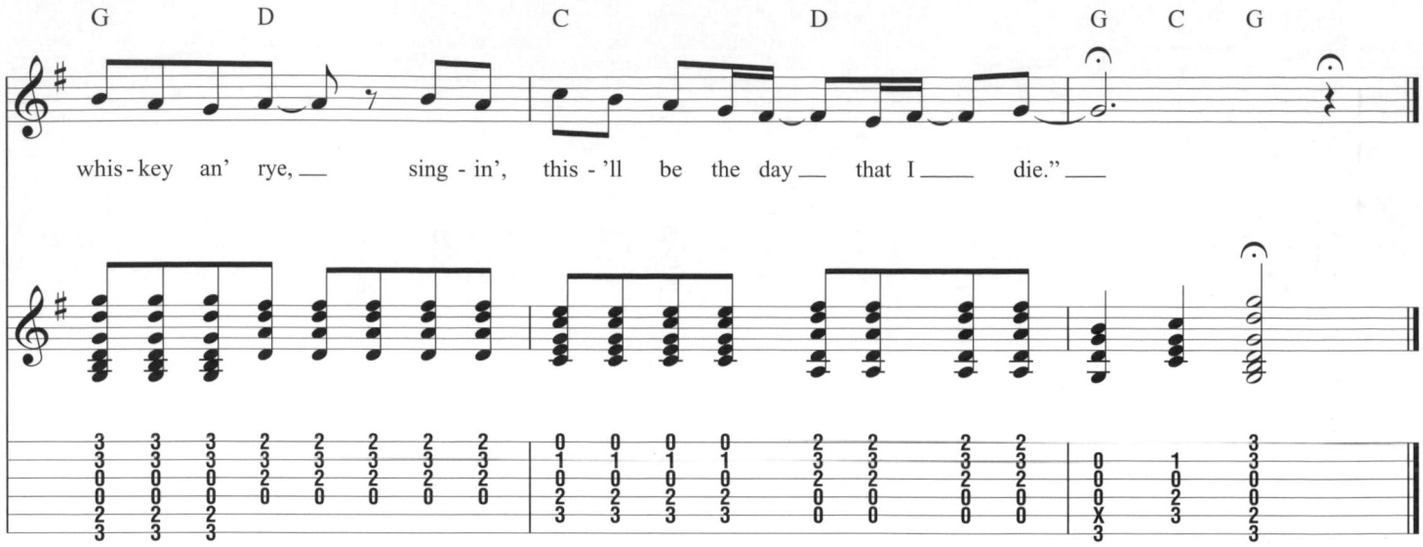

Additional Lyrics

2. Now for ten years we've been on our own, and moss grows fat on a rollin' stone.
   But, that's not how it used to be.
   When the jester sang for the king and queen in a coat he borrowed from James Dean,
   And a voice that came from you and me.
   Oh, and while the king was looking down, the jester stole his thorny crown.
   The courtroom was adjourned; no verdict was returned.
   And while Lenin read a book on Marx, the quartet practiced in the park,
   And we sang dirges in the dark the day the music died.
   We were singin',...

4. Oh, and there we were all in one place, a generation lost in space,
   With no time left to start again.
   So come on, Jack be nimble, Jack be quick! Jack Flash sat on a candlestick,
   'Cause fire is the devil's only friend.
   Oh, and as I watched him on the stage, my hands were clenched in fists of rage.
   No angel born in hell could break that Satan's spell.
   And as the flames climbed high into the night to light the sacrificial rite,
   I saw Satan laughing with delight the day the music died.
   He was singin',...

Baby, I Love Your Way

Words and Music by Peter Frampton

Copyright © 1975 ALMO MUSIC CORP. and NUAGES ARTISTS MUSIC LTD.
Copyright Renewed
All Rights Controlled and Administered by ALMO MUSIC CORP.
All Rights Reserved Used by Permission

C
F9
mov-ing
a - cross the page.
G
Dadd4/F♯
Em
Dadd4
Sud-den - ly
the day turns
in - to night
far a -
C
F9
way
from the cit - y.
But
Pre-Chorus
Bm7
E7
don't
hes - i - tate,
'cause your

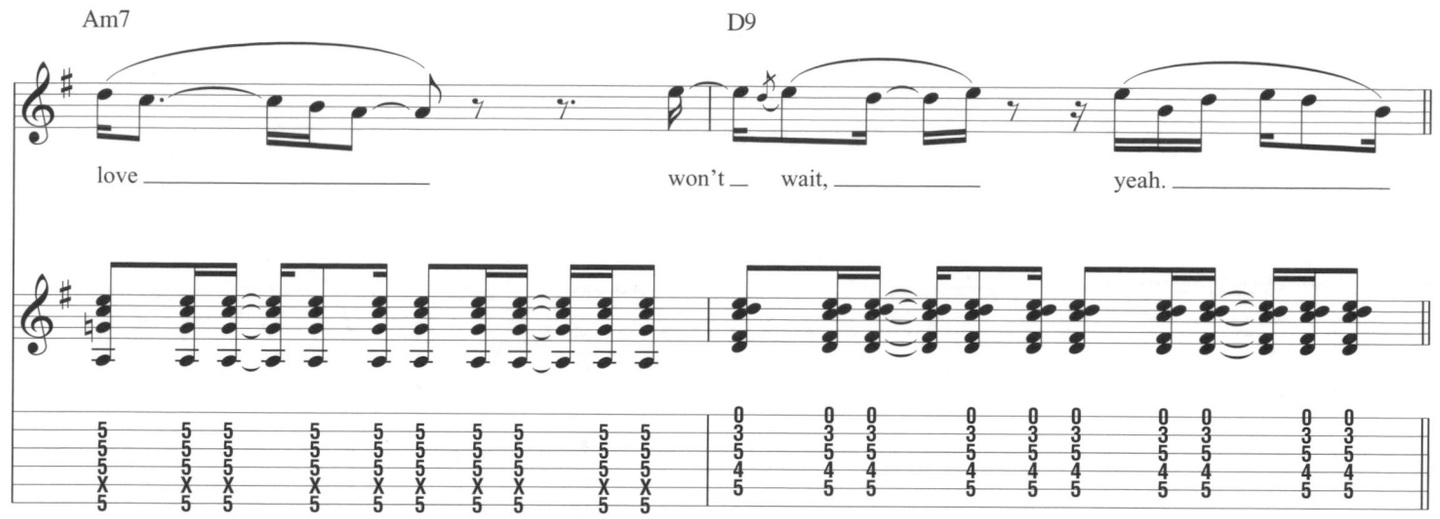

Chorus

To Coda 2

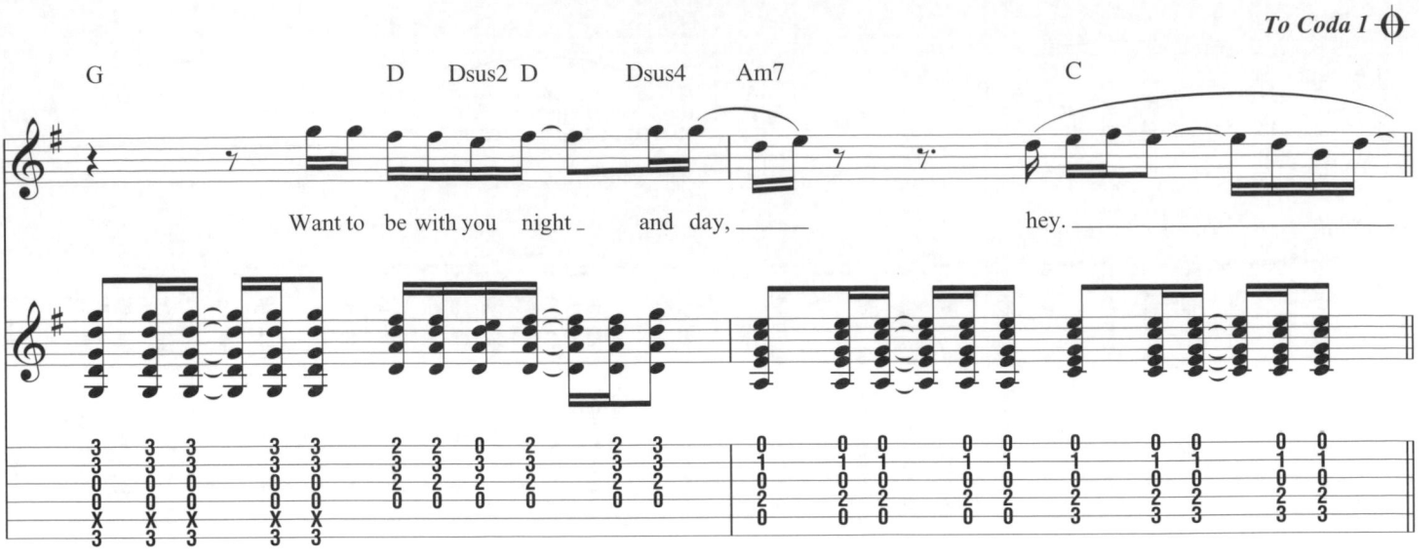

Interlude

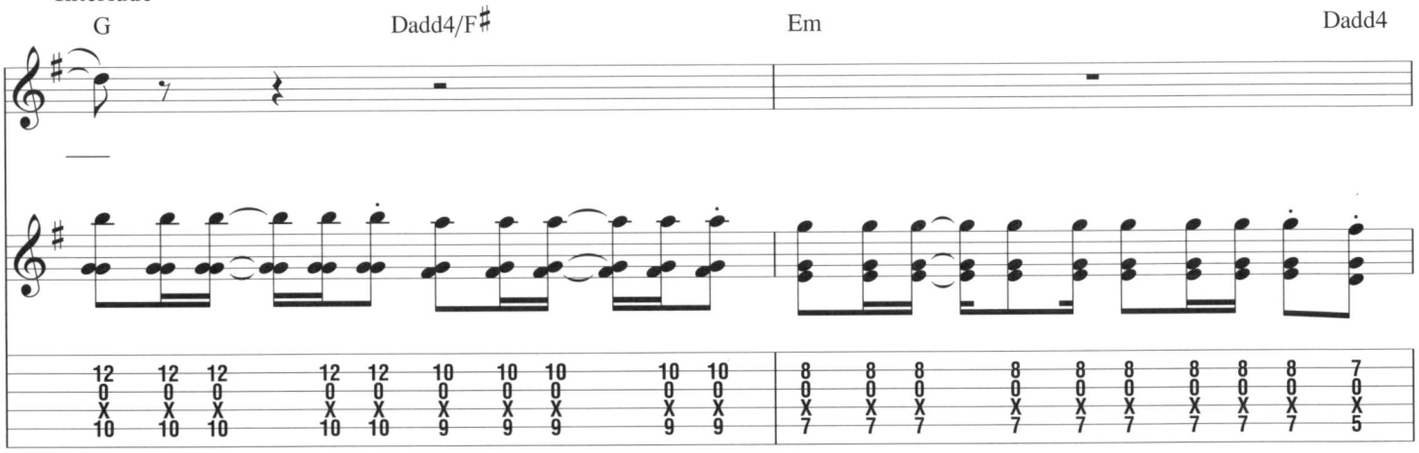

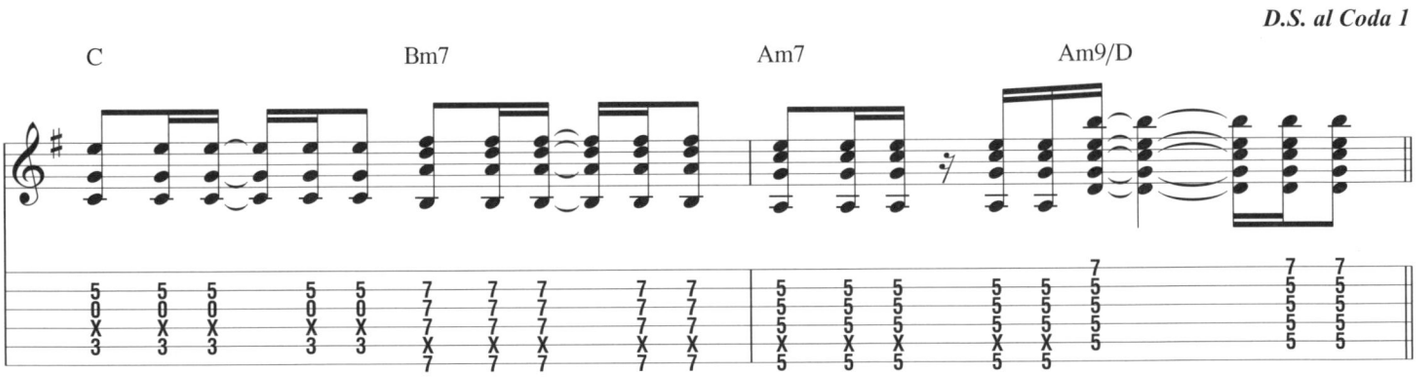

Coda 1

Electric Piano Solo

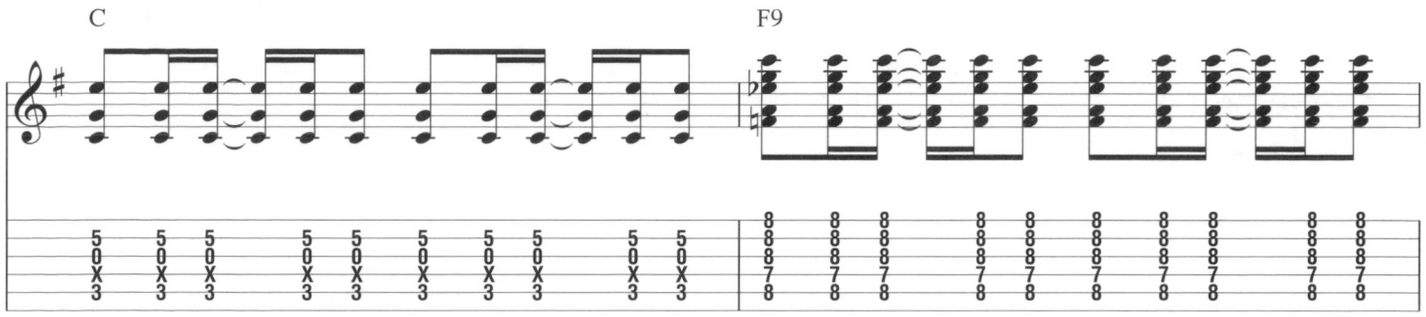

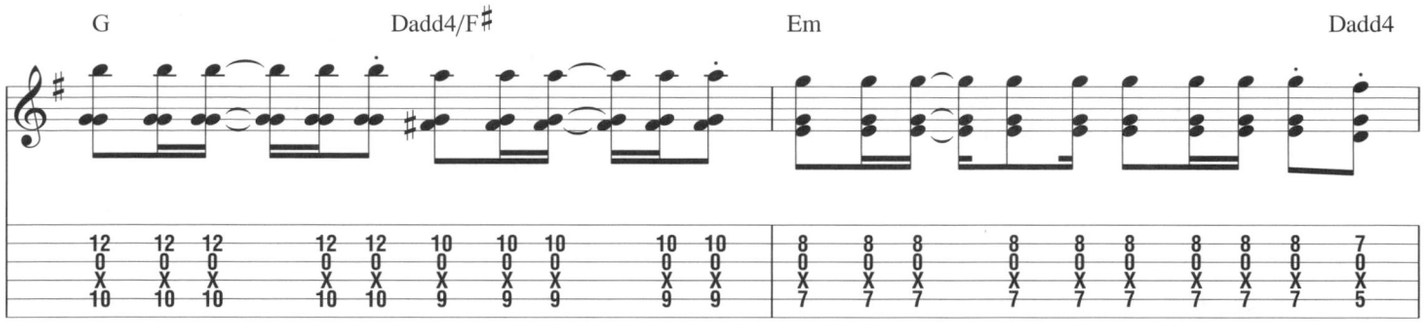

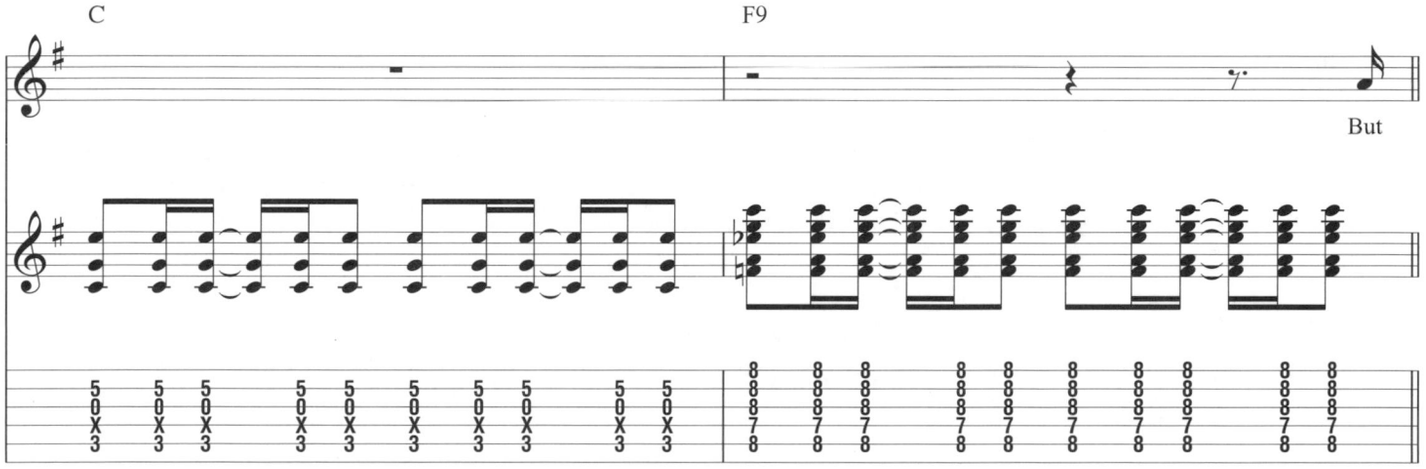

Pre-Chorus

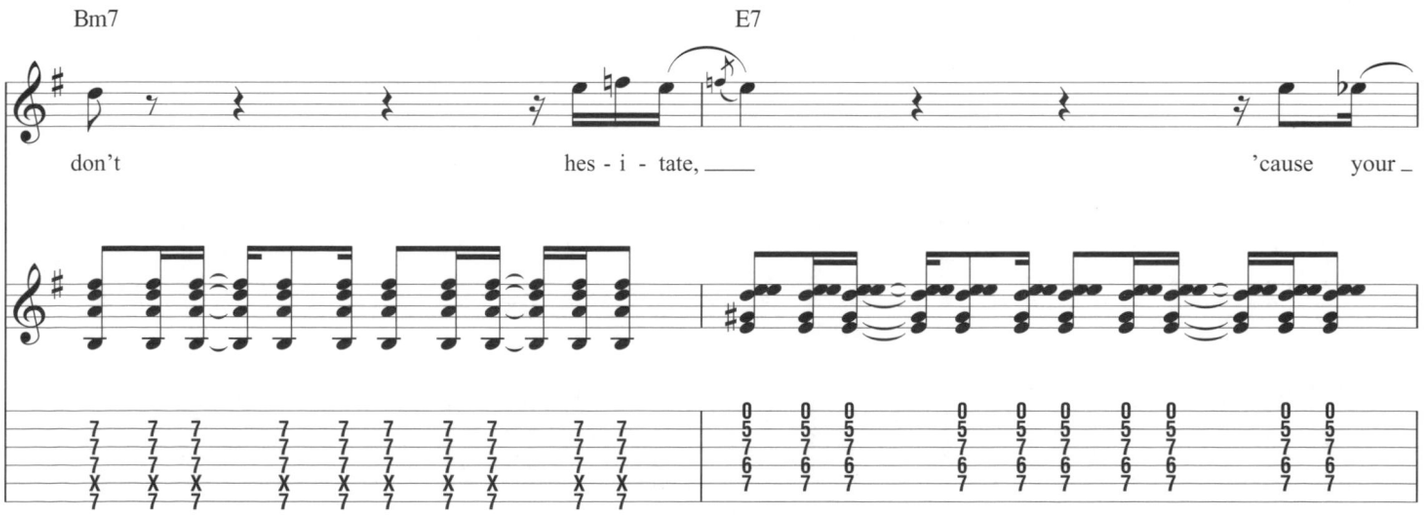

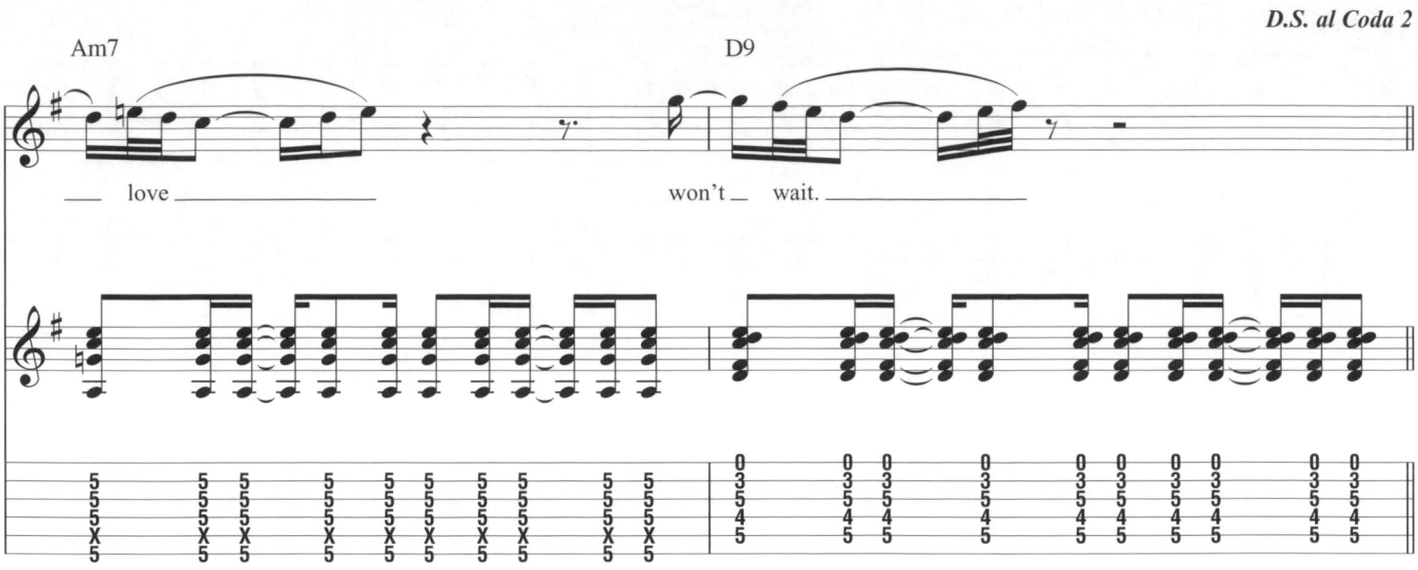
D.S. al Coda 2
Am7
D9
love
won't wait.

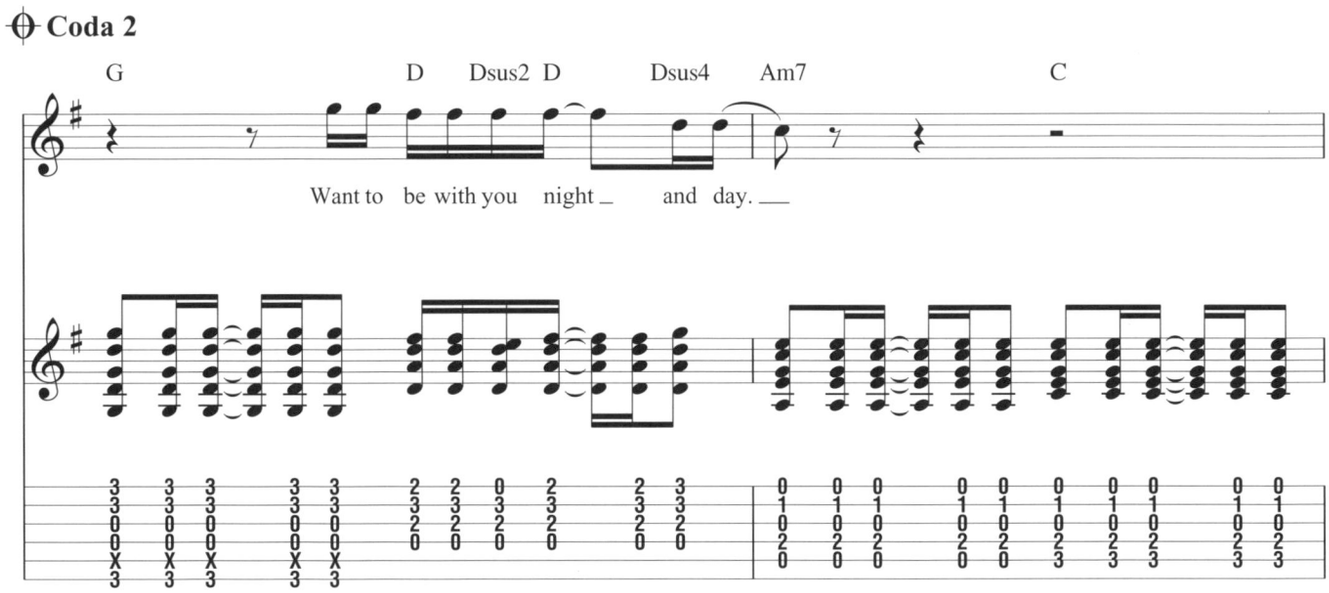
Coda 2
G
D Dsus2 D
Dsus4
Am7
C
Want to be with you night and day.

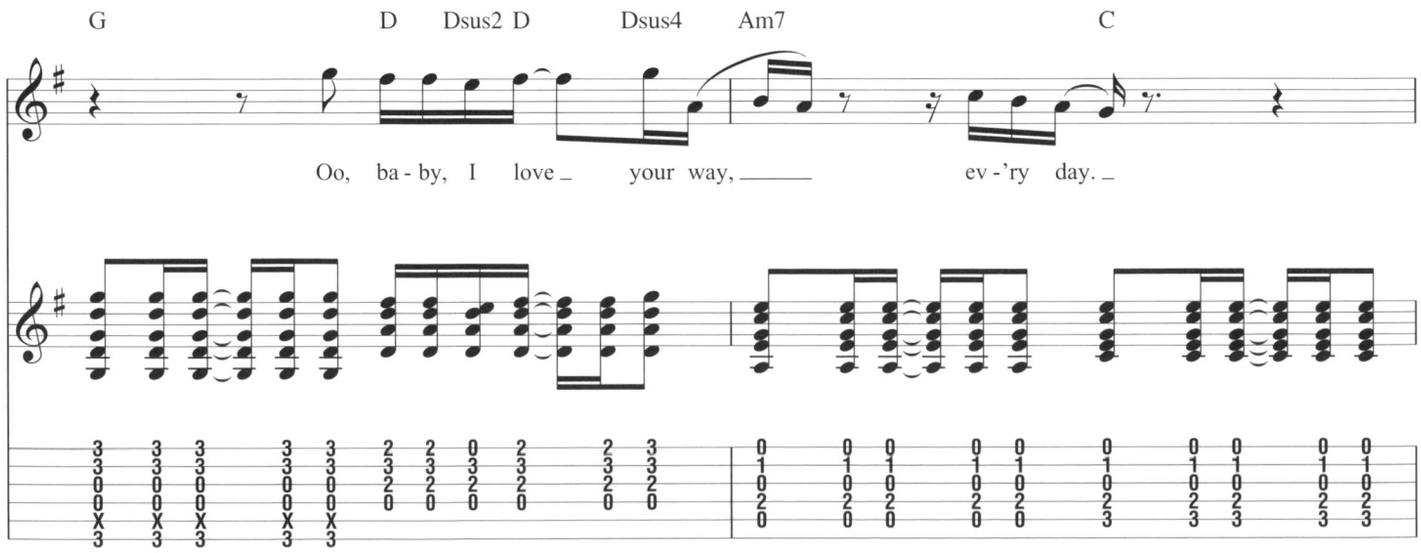
G
D Dsus2 D
Dsus4
Am7
C
Oo, ba - by, I love your way,
ev - 'ry day.

Outro

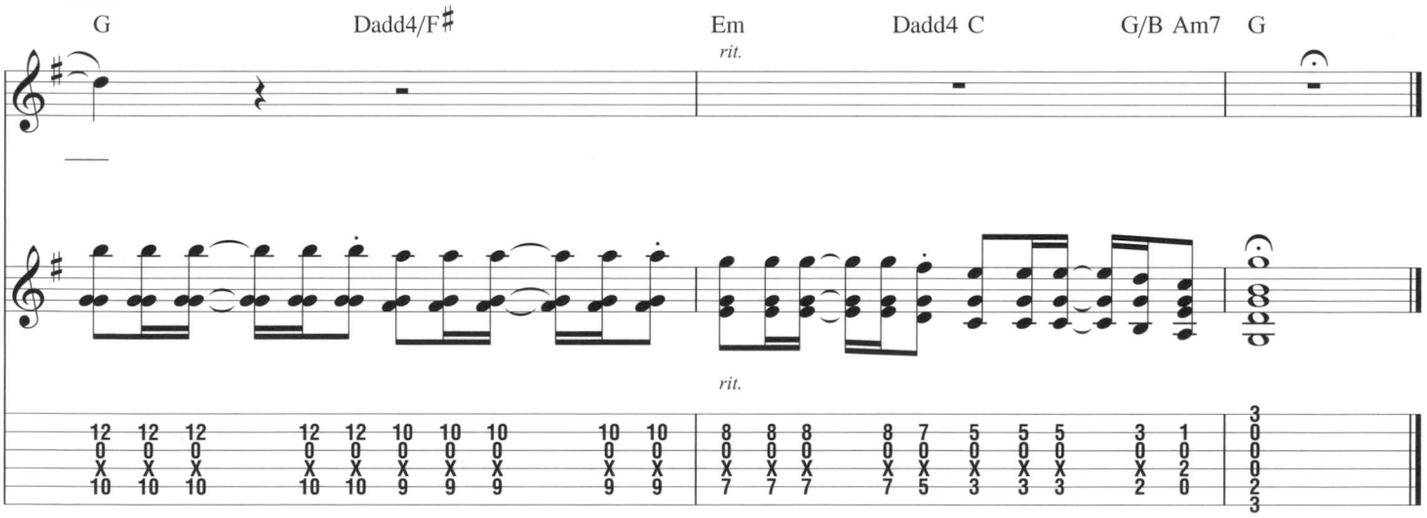

Additional Lyrics

2. Moon appears to shine and light the sky
With the help of some firefly.
I wonder how they have the power to shine, shine, shine.
I can see them under the pine.

3. I can see the sunset in your eyes,
Brown and grey, and blue besides.
Clouds are stalking islands in the sun.
Wish I could buy one out of season.

Barely Breathing

Words and Music by Duncan Sheik

Copyright © 1996 by Universal Music - Careers, Duncan Sheik Songs and Happ-Dog Music
All Rights Administered by Universal Music - Careers
International Copyright Secured All Rights Reserved

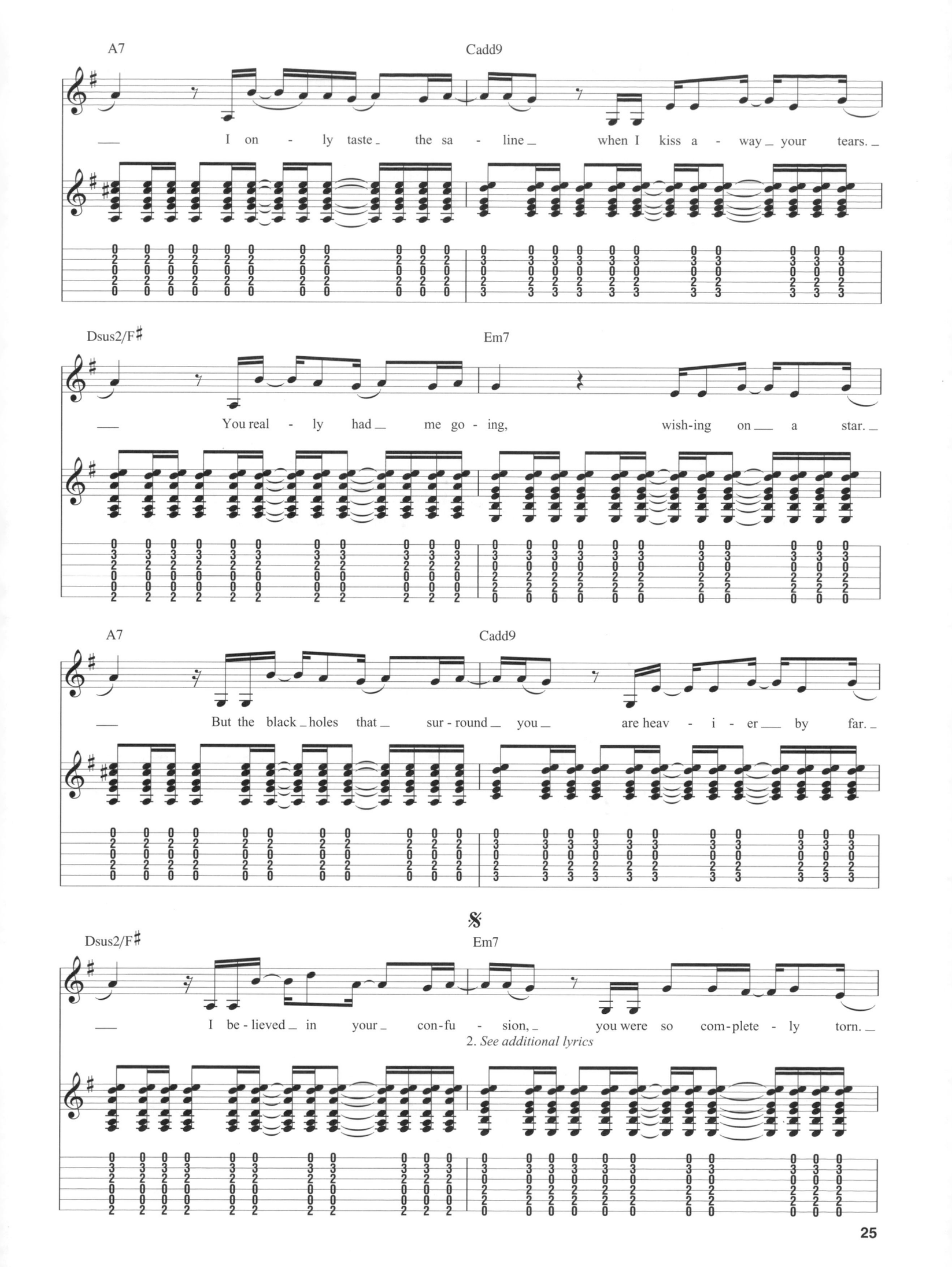
A7
Cadd9
I on - ly taste the sa - line when I kiss a - way your tears.
Dsus2/F♯
Em7
You real - ly had me go - ing, wish-ing on a star.
A7
Cadd9
But the black holes that sur - round you are heav - i - er by far.
𝄋
Dsus2/F♯
Em7
I be - lieved in your con-fu - sion, you were so com-plete - ly torn.
2. See additional lyrics

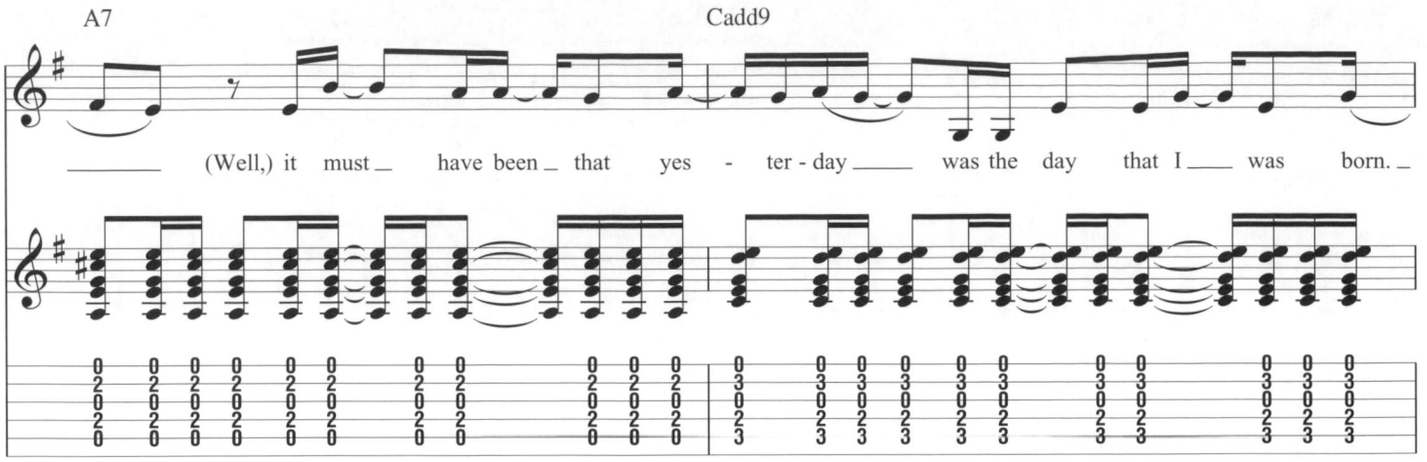
A7
Cadd9
(Well,) it must have been that yes - ter - day was the day that I was born.

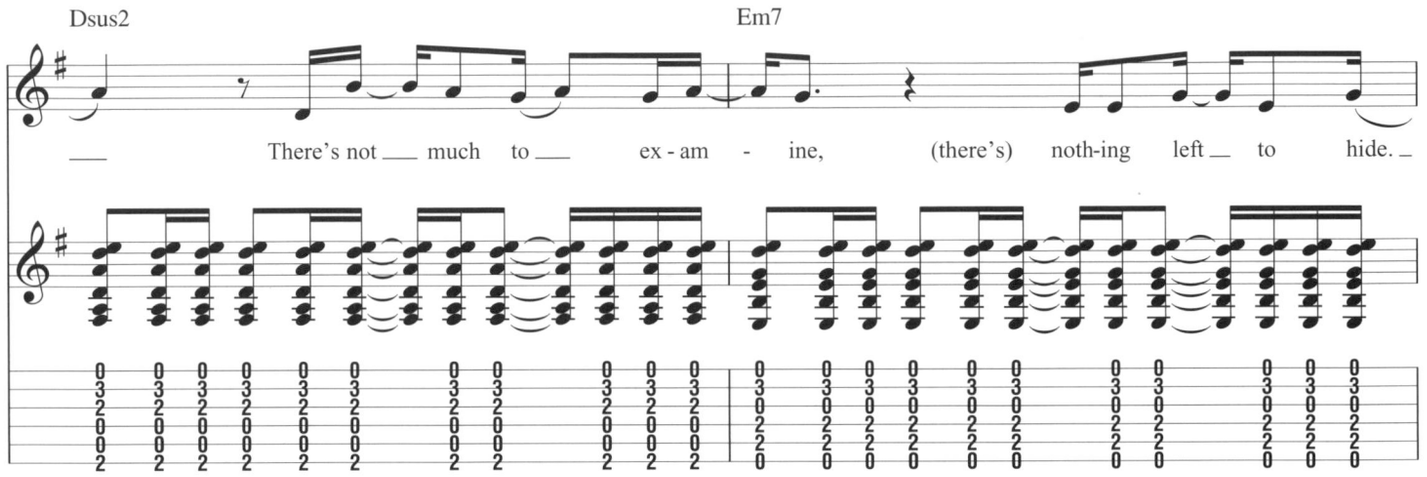
Dsus2
Em7
There's not much to ex - am - ine, (there's) noth-ing left to hide.

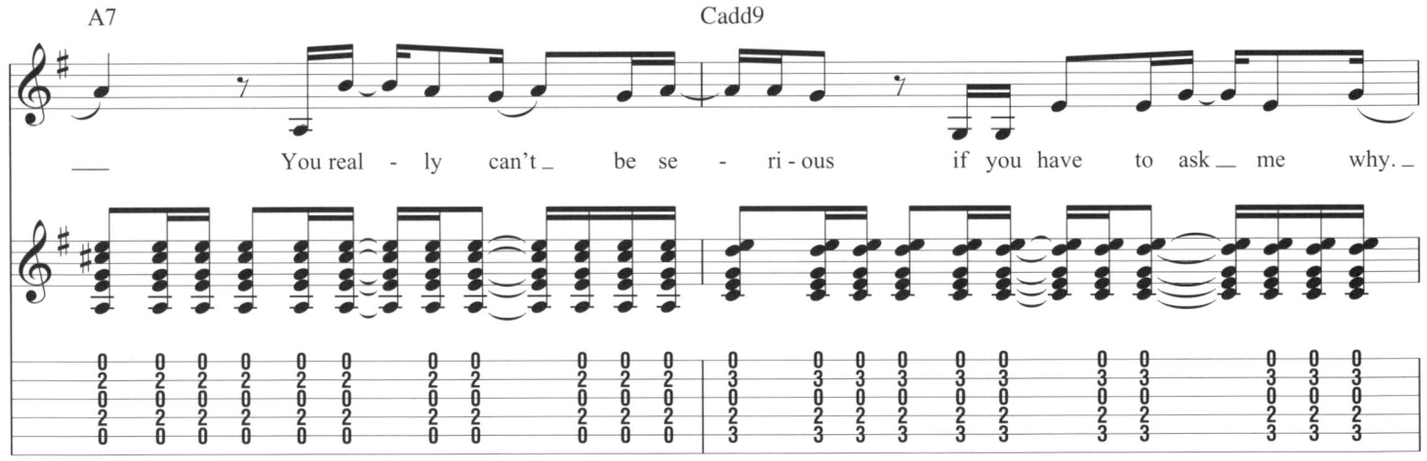
A7
Cadd9
You real - ly can't be se - ri - ous if you have to ask me why.

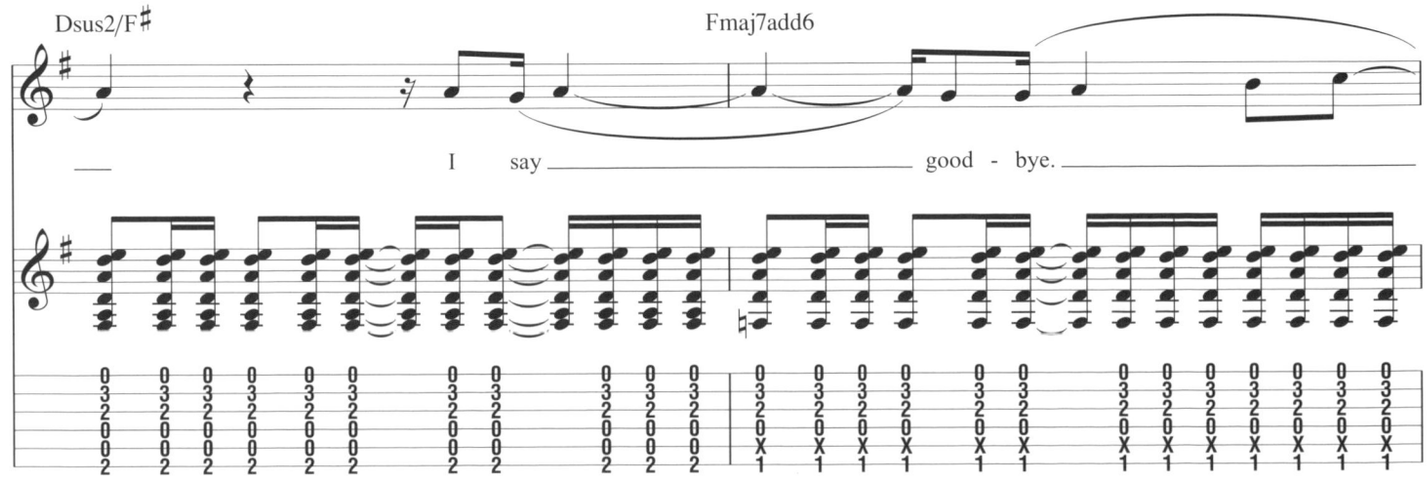
Dsus2/F♯
Fmaj7add6
I say good - bye.

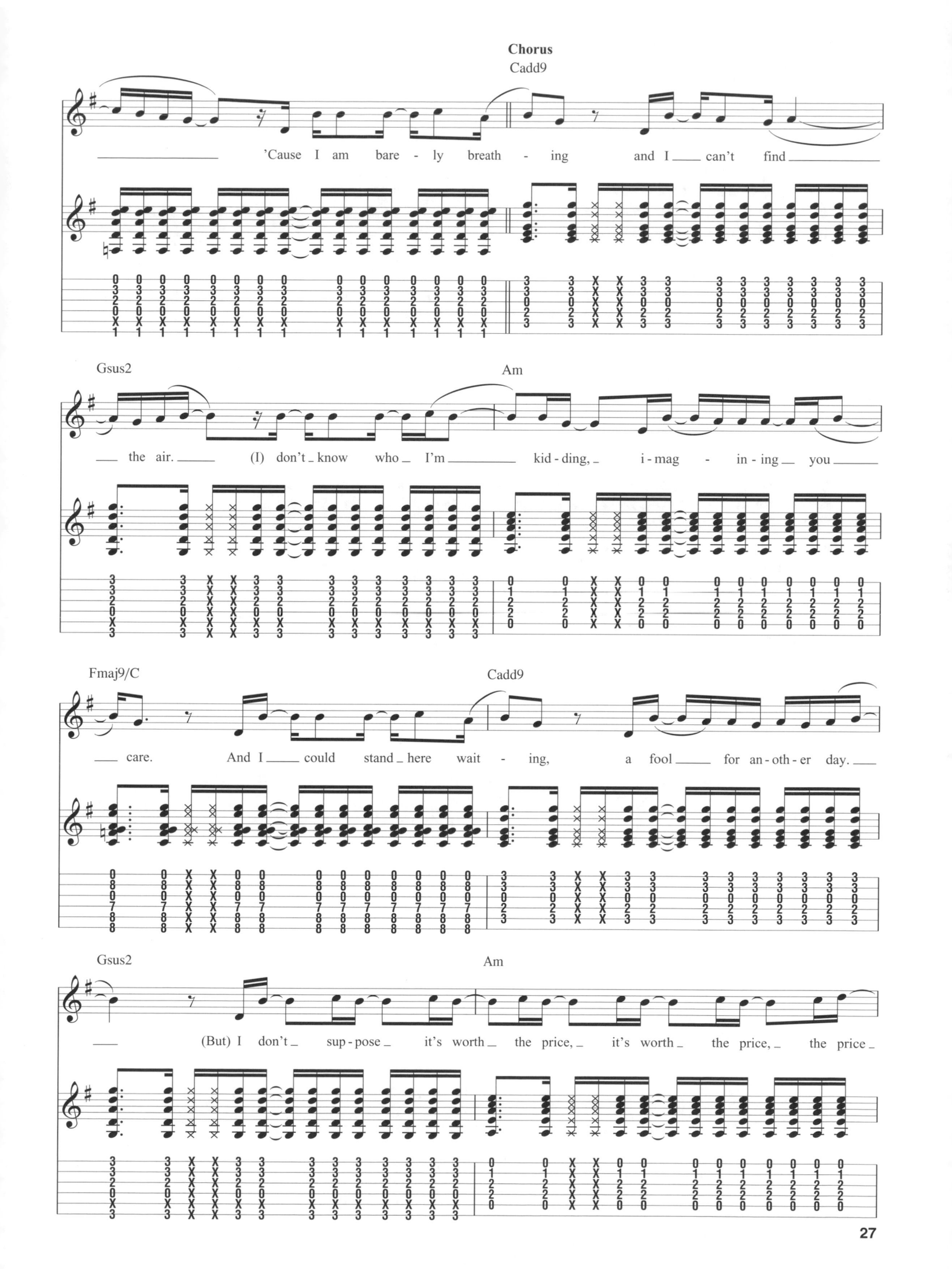
Chorus
Cadd9
'Cause I am bare - ly breath - ing and I can't find
Gsus2
Am
the air. (I) don't know who I'm kid - ding, i - mag - in - ing you
Fmaj9/C
Cadd9
care. And I could stand here wait - ing, a fool for an - oth - er day.
Gsus2
Am
(But) I don't sup - pose it's worth the price, it's worth the price, the price

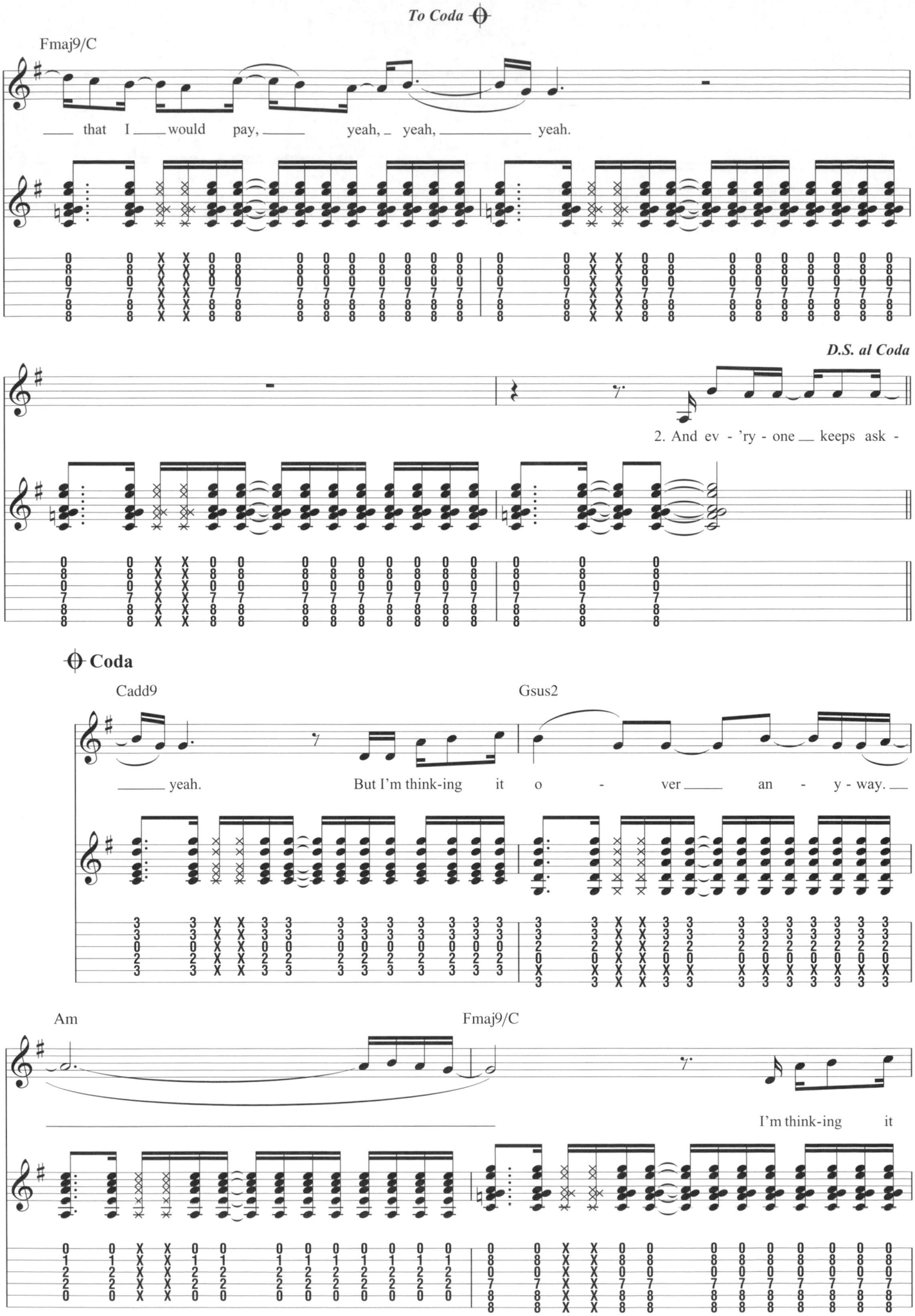
To Coda
Fmaj9/C
that I would pay, yeah, yeah, yeah.
D.S. al Coda
2. And ev - 'ry - one keeps ask -
Coda
Cadd9
Gsus2
yeah. But I'm think-ing it o - ver an - y - way.
Am
Fmaj9/C
I'm think-ing it

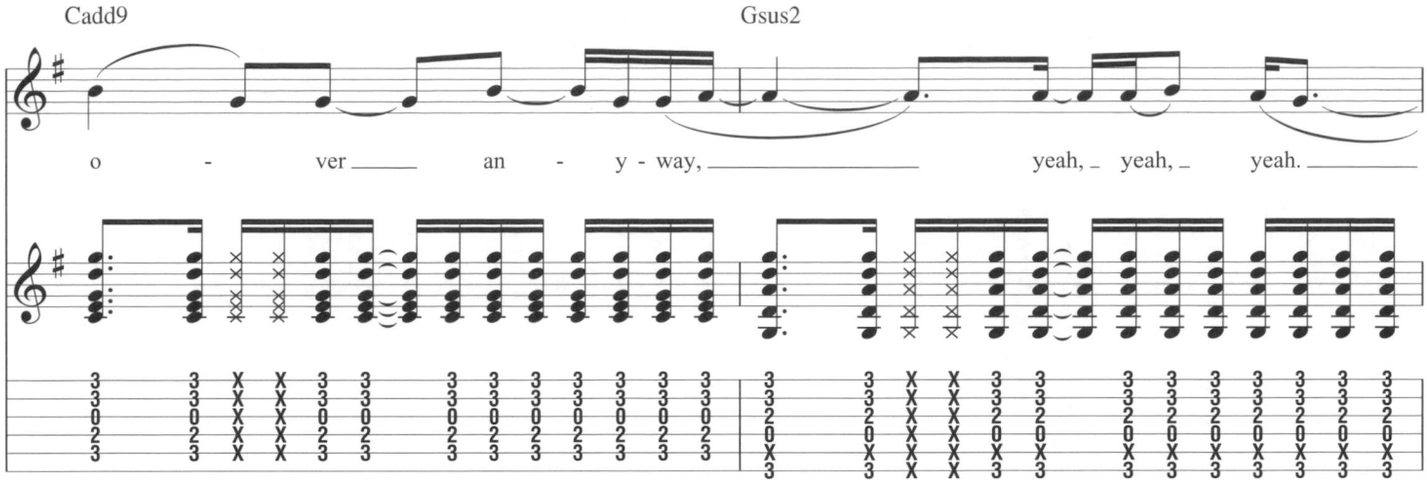
Cadd9
Gsus2
o - ver an - y - way, yeah, yeah, yeah.

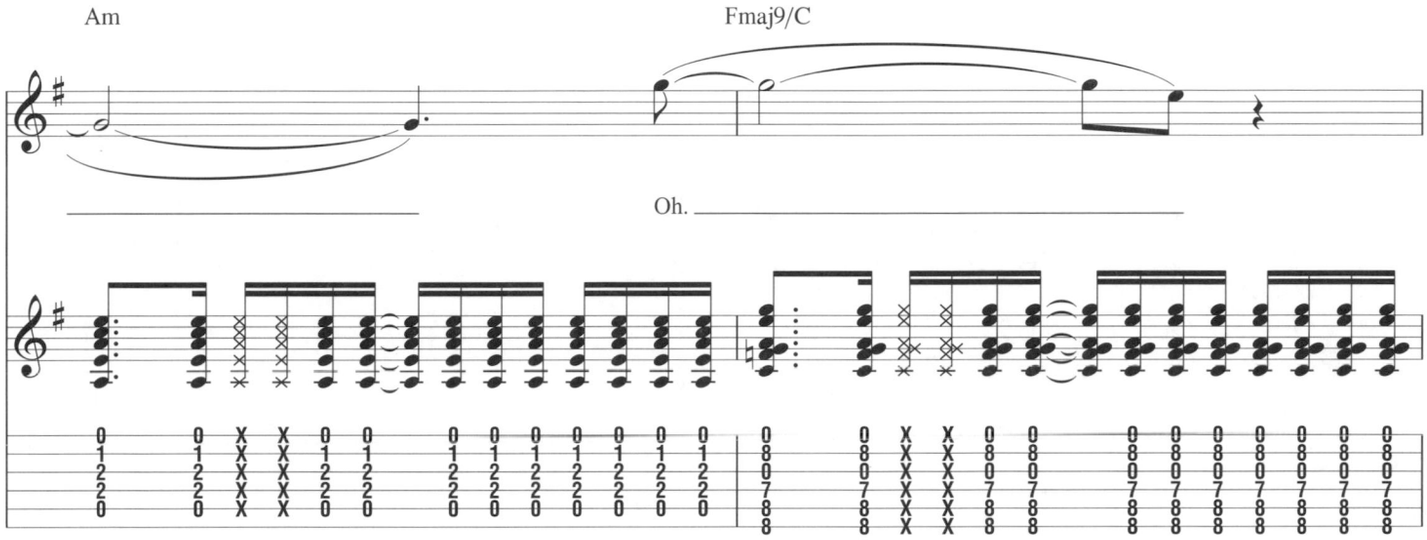
Am
Fmaj9/C
Oh.

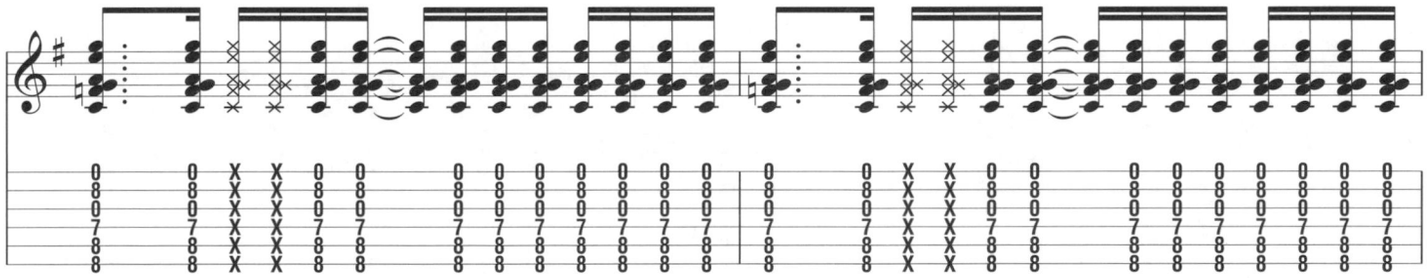

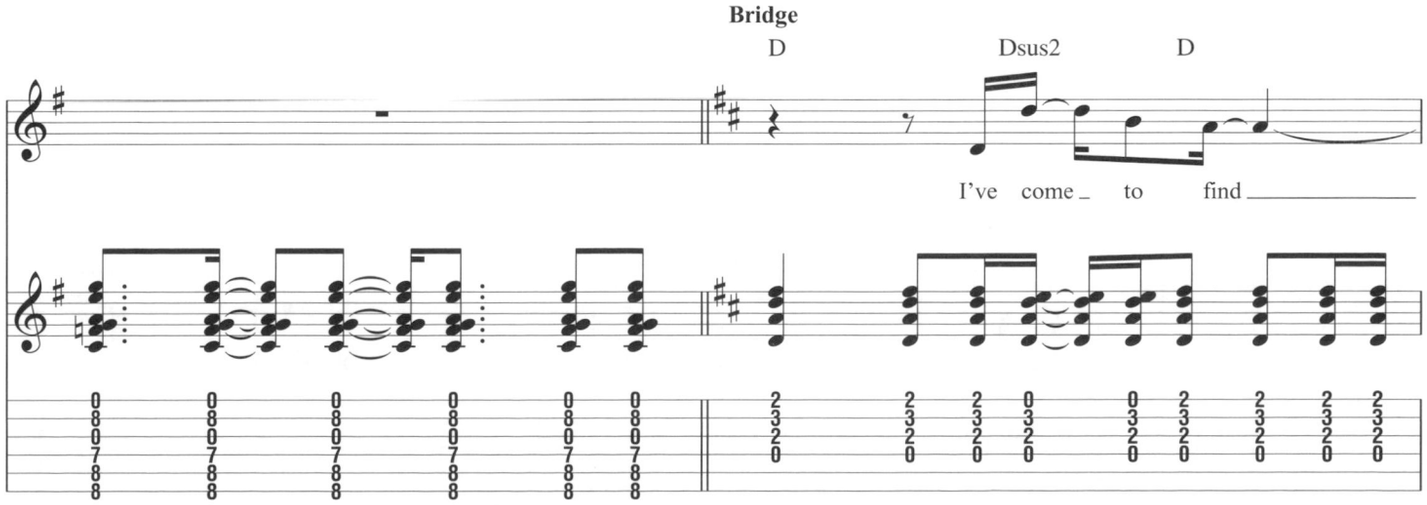
Bridge
D
Dsus2
D
I've come to find

Am
Am7
Am
Am7
Cadd9
I may nev - er know
your chang - ing mind.
Gm13
D
Is it friend or foe?
I rise a - bove
Am
Am7
Am
Am7
Cadd9
or sink be - low
with ev - 'ry time
Gm13
you come and go.
Please, don't

Outro-Chorus

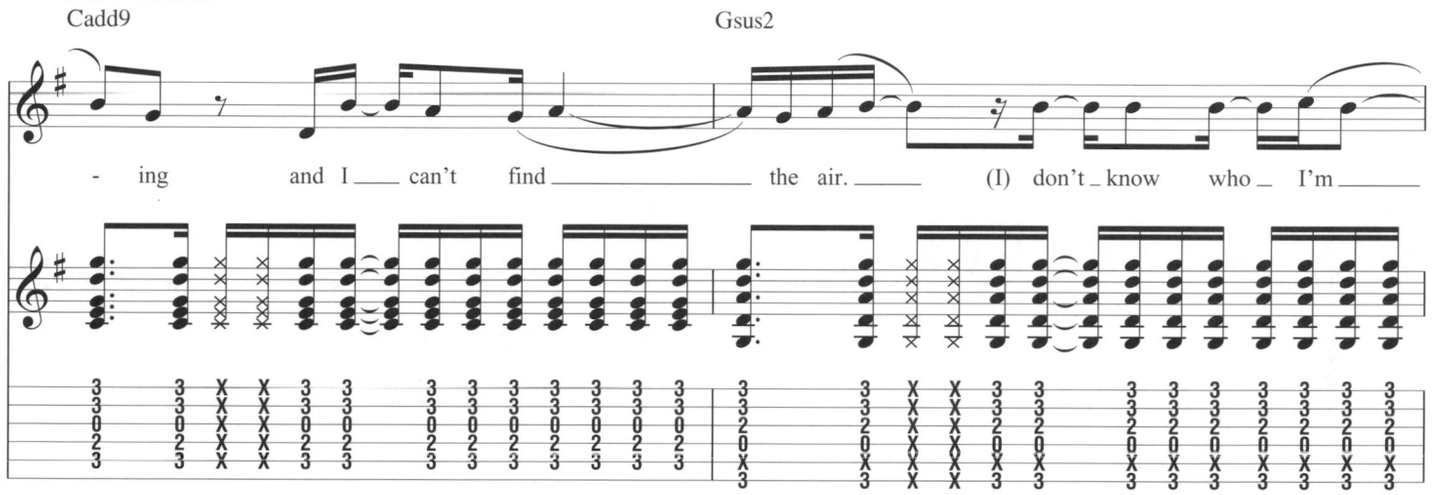

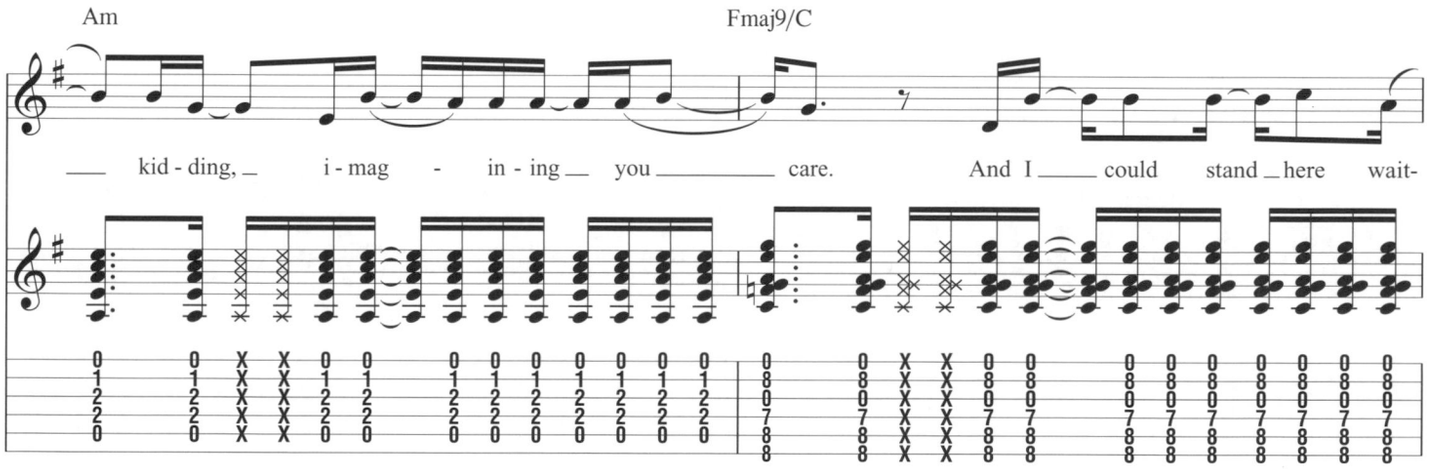

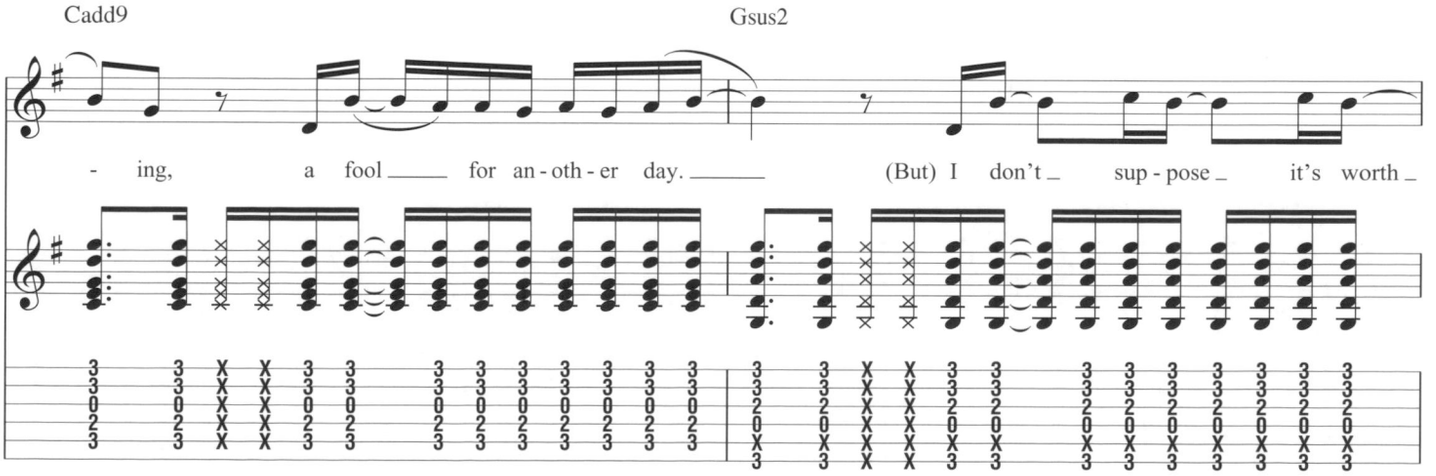

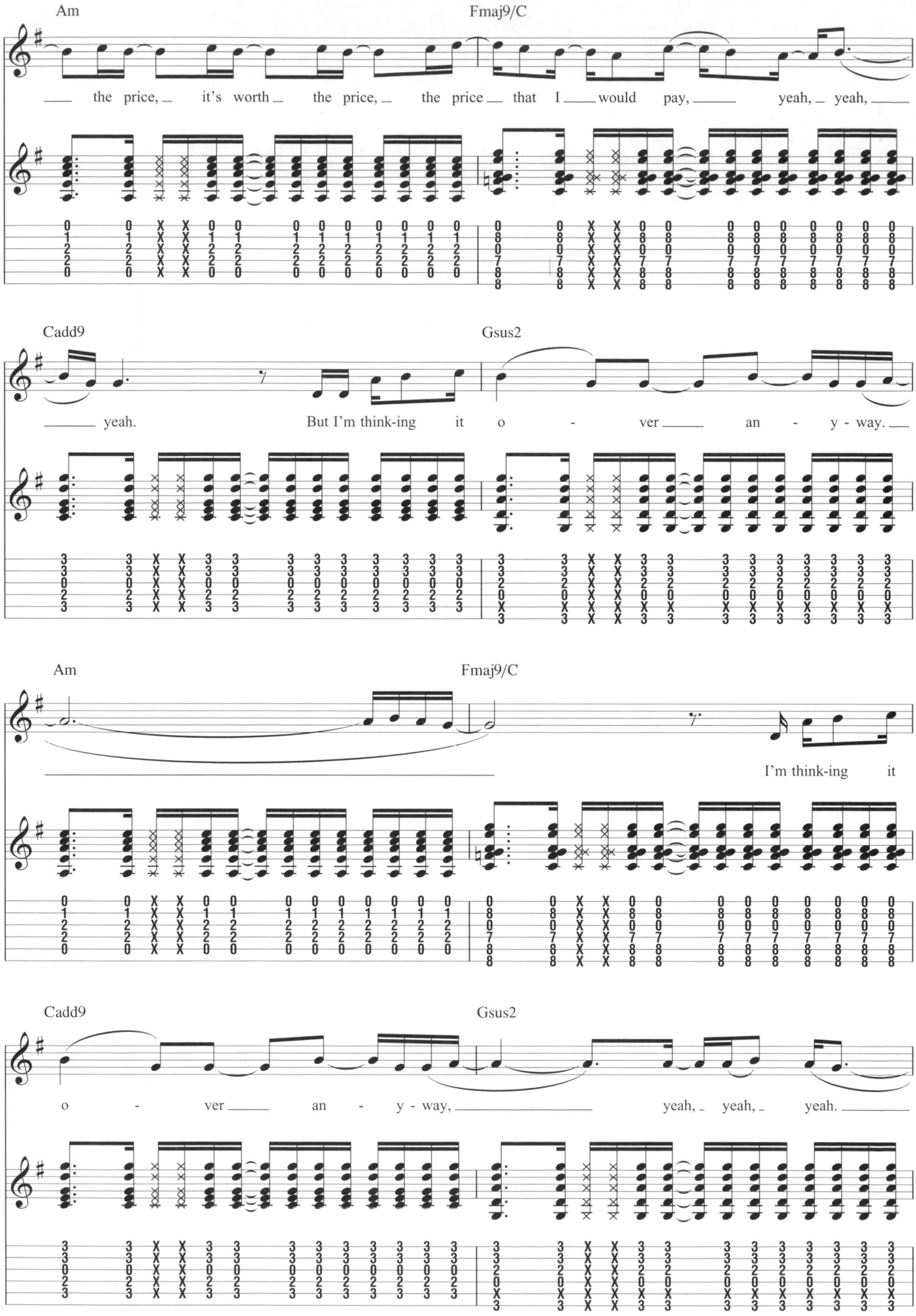
Am
Fmaj9/C
the price, it's worth the price, the price that I would pay, yeah, yeah,
Cadd9
Gsus2
yeah. But I'm think-ing it o - ver an - y - way.
Am
Fmaj9/C
I'm think-ing it
Cadd9
Gsus2
o - ver an - y - way, yeah, yeah, yeah.

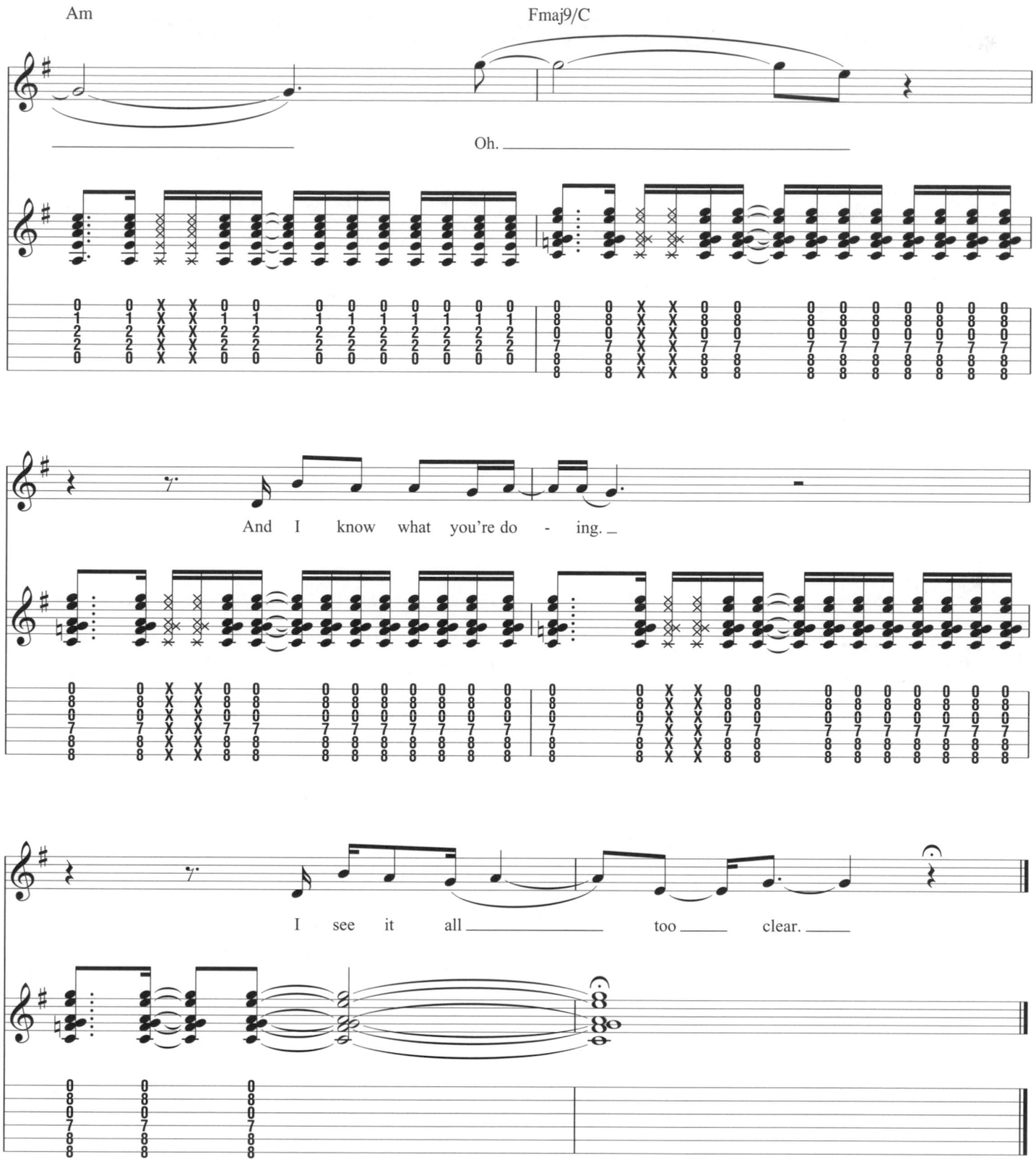

Additional Lyrics

2. And ev'ryone keeps asking, "What's it all about?"
I used to be so certain; now I can't figure out.
What is this attraction? I only feel the pain.
And nothing left to reason, and only you to blame.
Will it ever change?

Boulevard of Broken Dreams

Words by Billie Joe
Music by Green Day

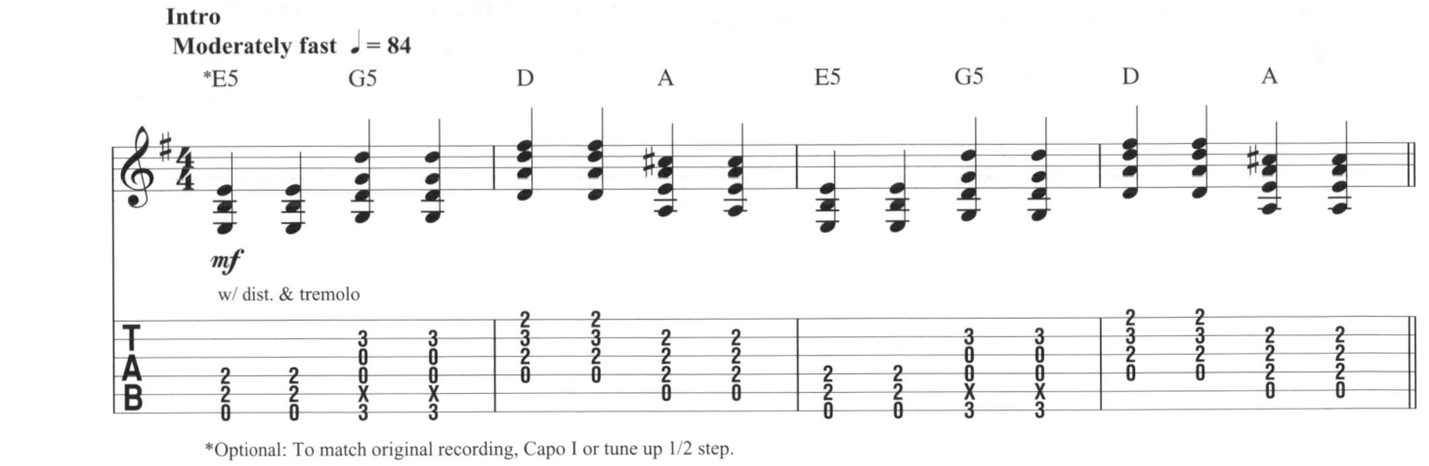

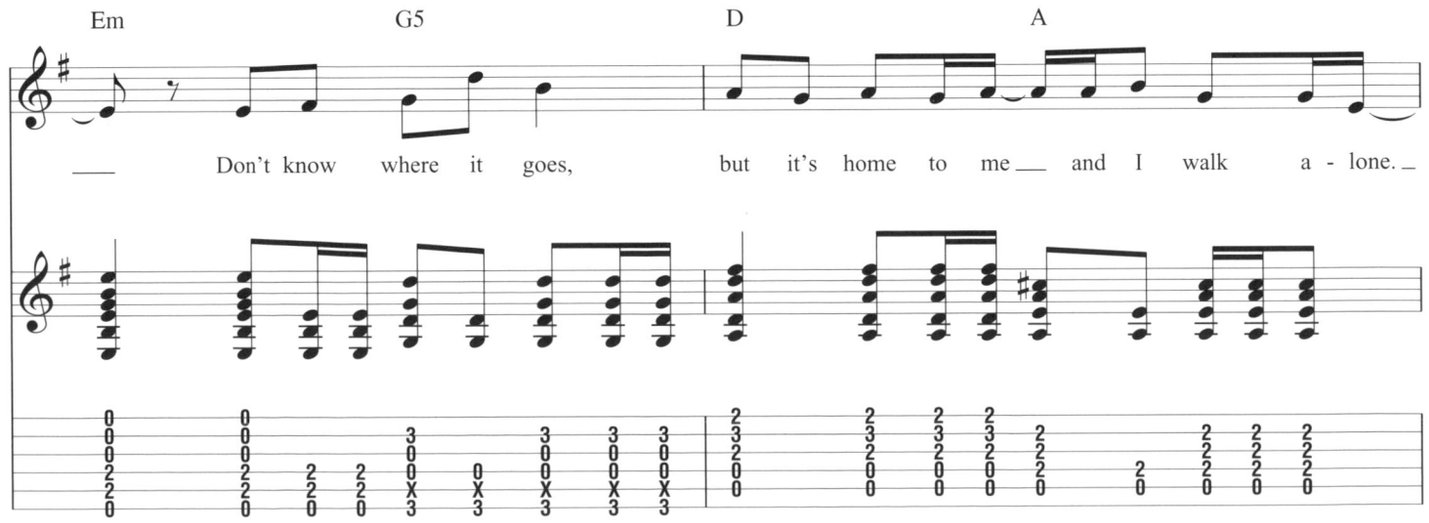

© 2004 WB MUSIC CORP. and GREEN DAZE MUSIC
All Rights Administered by WB MUSIC CORP.
All Rights Reserved Used by Permission

Em G5 D A
I walk this emp - ty street on the bou - le - vard of bro - ken dreams,
Em G5 D A
when the cit - y sleeps and I'm the on - ly one and I walk a - lone.
Em G5 D A
I walk a - lone, I walk a - lone.

Em
G5
D
A5
B5
I walk a - lone, I walk a...
w/ dist.
Chorus
C5
G5
D5
E5
My shad - ow's (the) on - ly one that walks be - side me.
C5
G5
D5
E5
My shal - low heart's the on - ly thing that's beat - ing.
C5
G5
D5
E5
Some - times I wish some - one up there will find me.

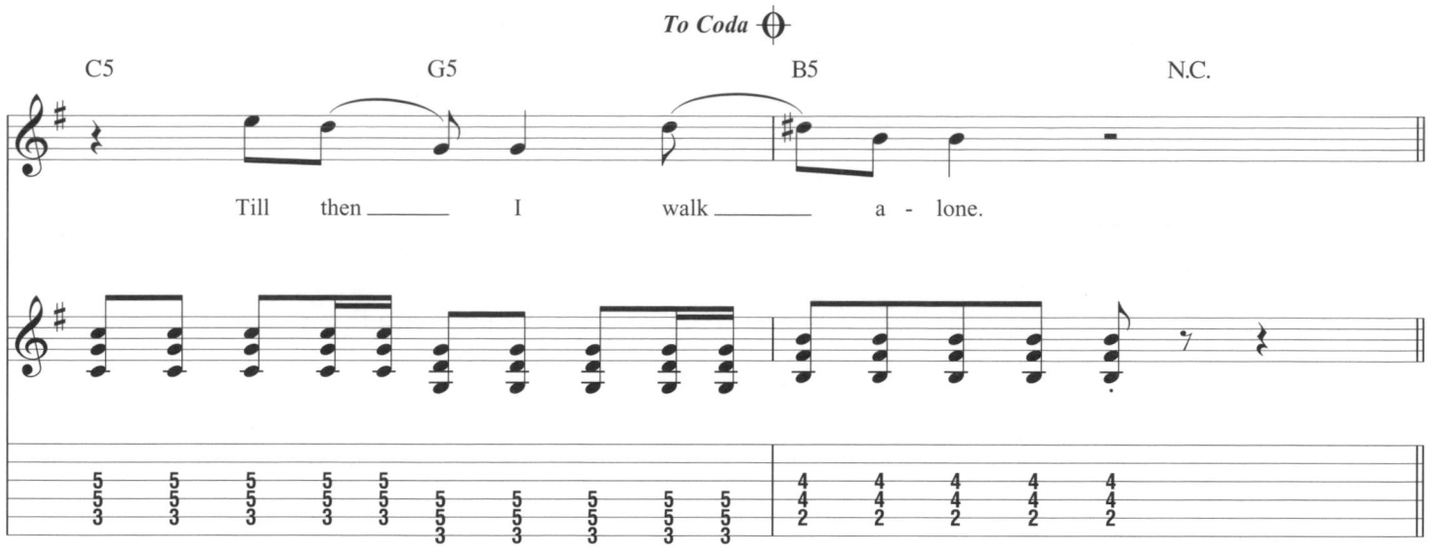
To Coda
C5
G5
B5
N.C.
Till then I walk a - lone.

Interlude

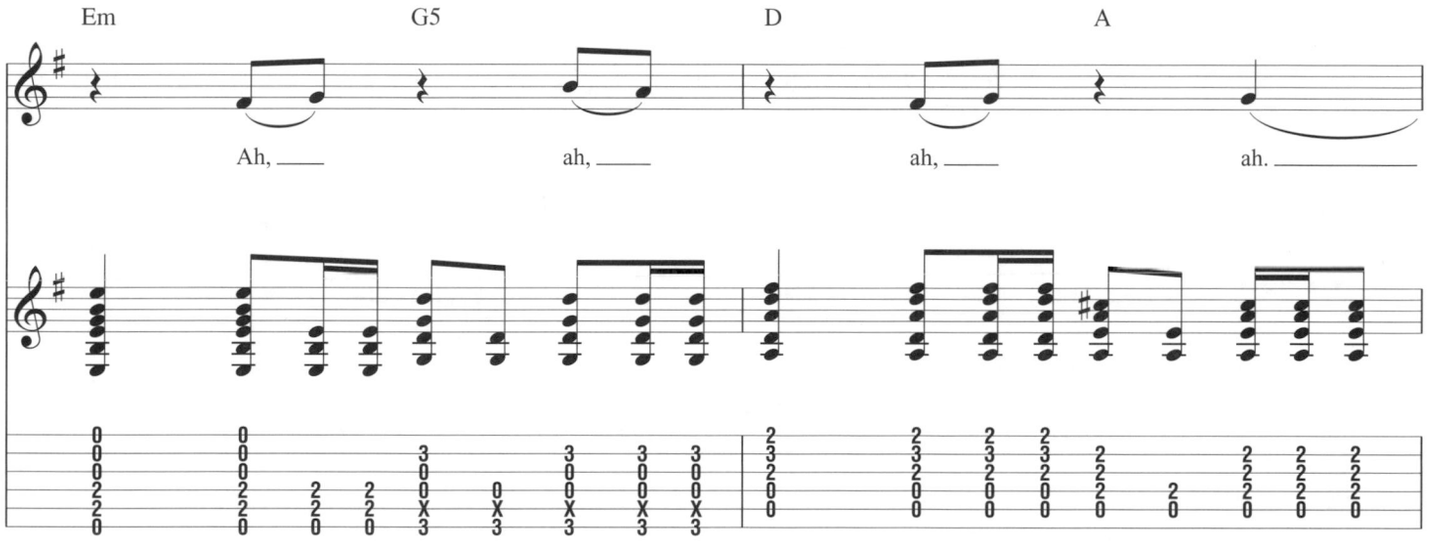
Em
G5
D
A
Ah, ah, ah, ah.

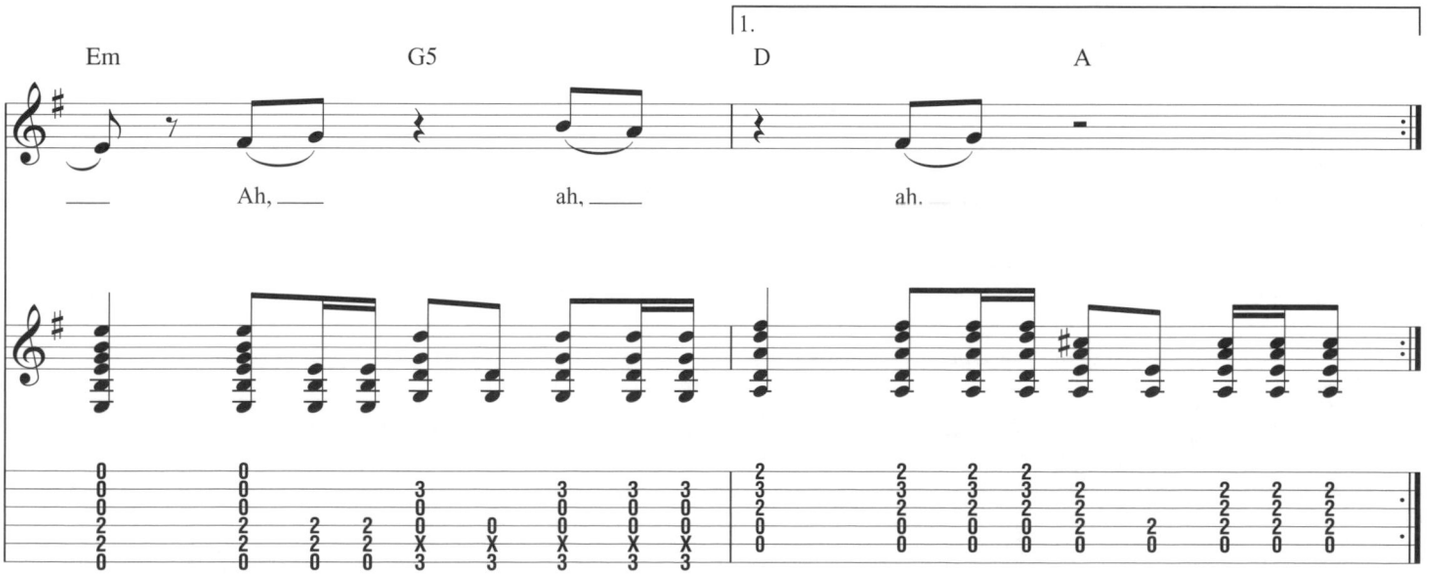
1.
Em
G5
D
A
Ah, ah, ah.

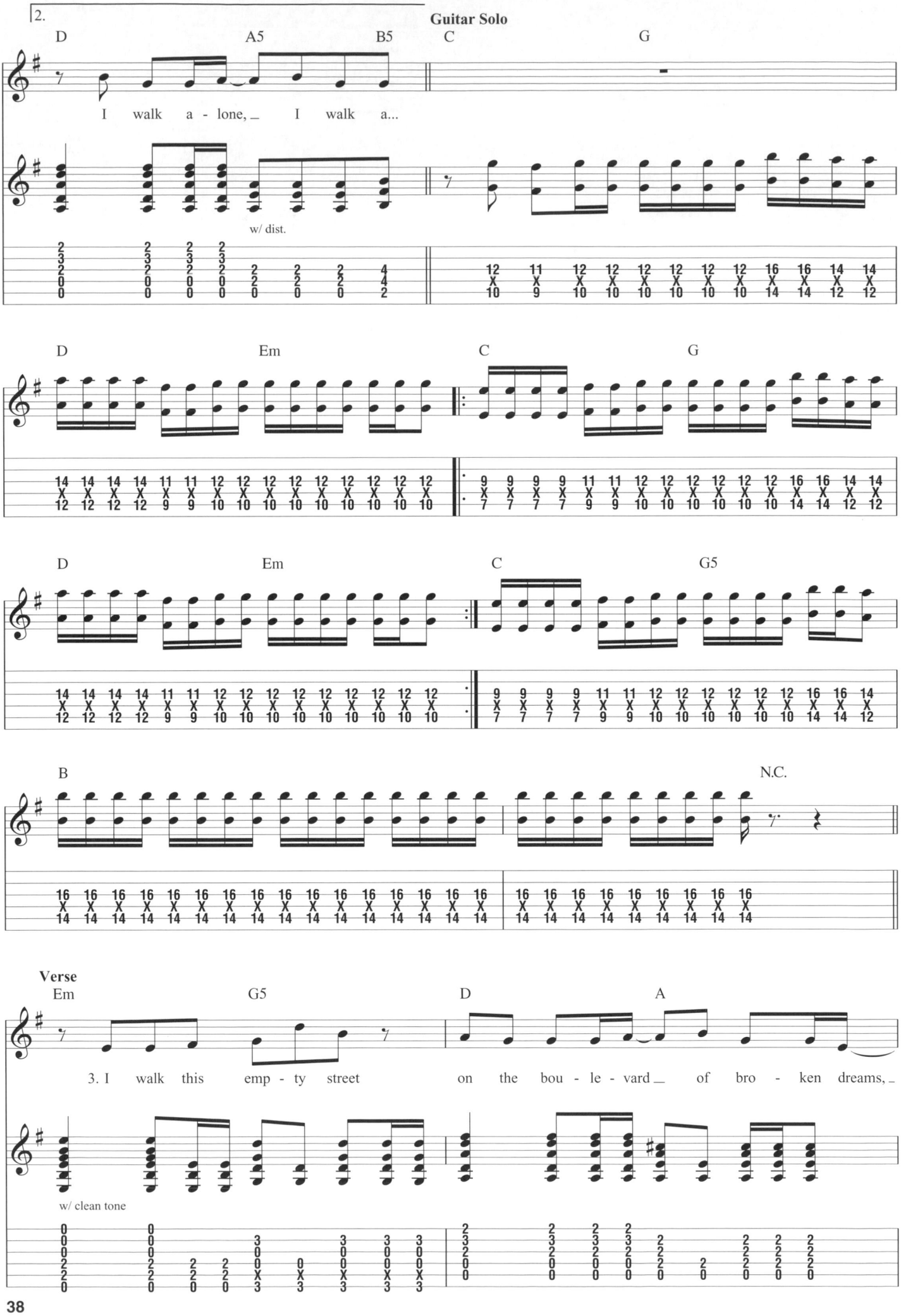
2.
Guitar Solo
D A5 B5 C G
I walk a - lone, I walk a...
w/ dist.
D Em C G
D Em C G5
B N.C.
Verse
Em G5 D A
3. I walk this emp - ty street on the bou - le - vard of bro - ken dreams,
w/ clean tone

Additional Lyrics

2. I'm walkin' down the line that divides me somewhere in my mind.
On the borderline of the edge and where I walk alone.
Read between the lines, what's fucked up and ev'rything's alright.
Check my vital signs to know I'm still alive and I walk alone.
I walk alone, I walk alone.
I walk alone, I walk a...

Chasing Cars

Words and Music by Gary Lightbody, Tom Simpson, Paul Wilson, Jonathan Quinn and Nathan Connolly

Copyright © 2006 UNIVERSAL MUSIC PUBLISHING BL LTD.
All Rights in the U.S. and Canada Controlled and Administered by UNIVERSAL - SONGS OF POLYGRAM INTERNATIONAL, INC.
All Rights Reserved Used by Permission

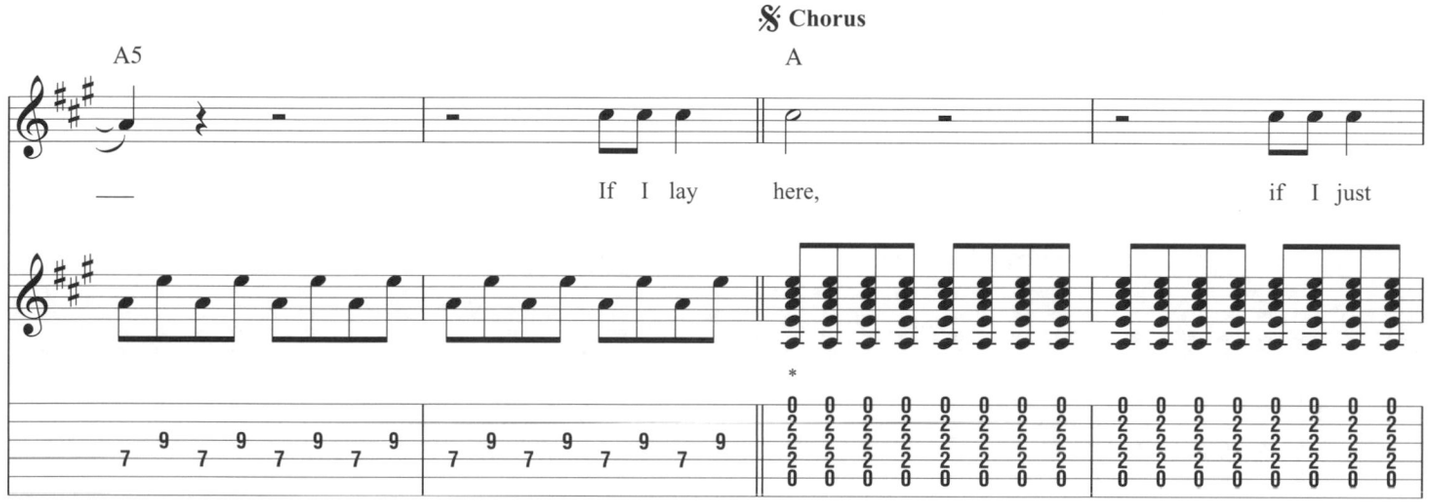

*3rd time, w/ dist.

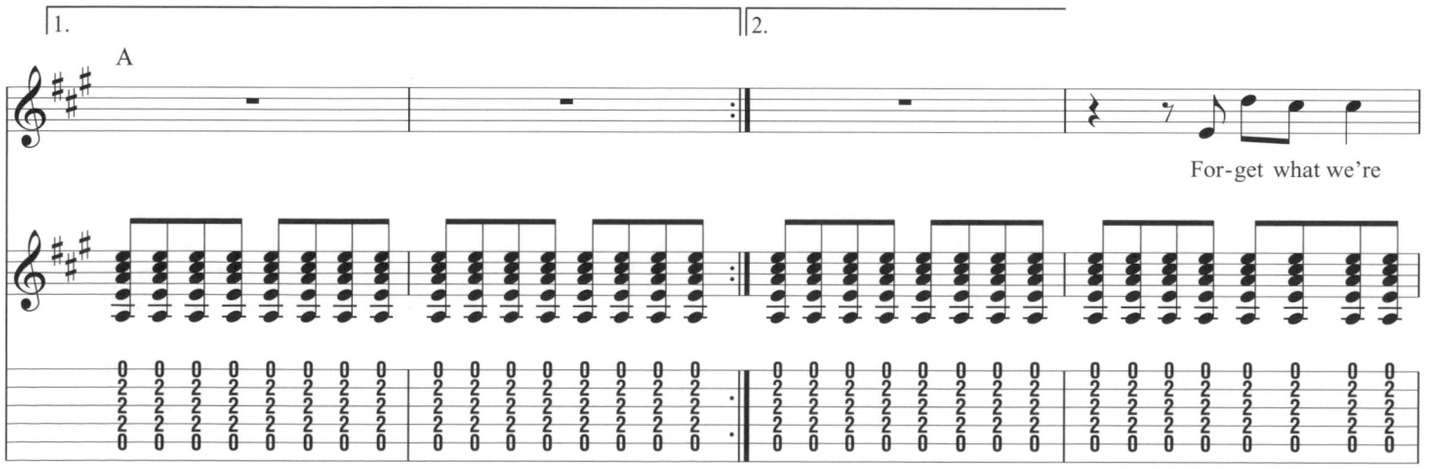

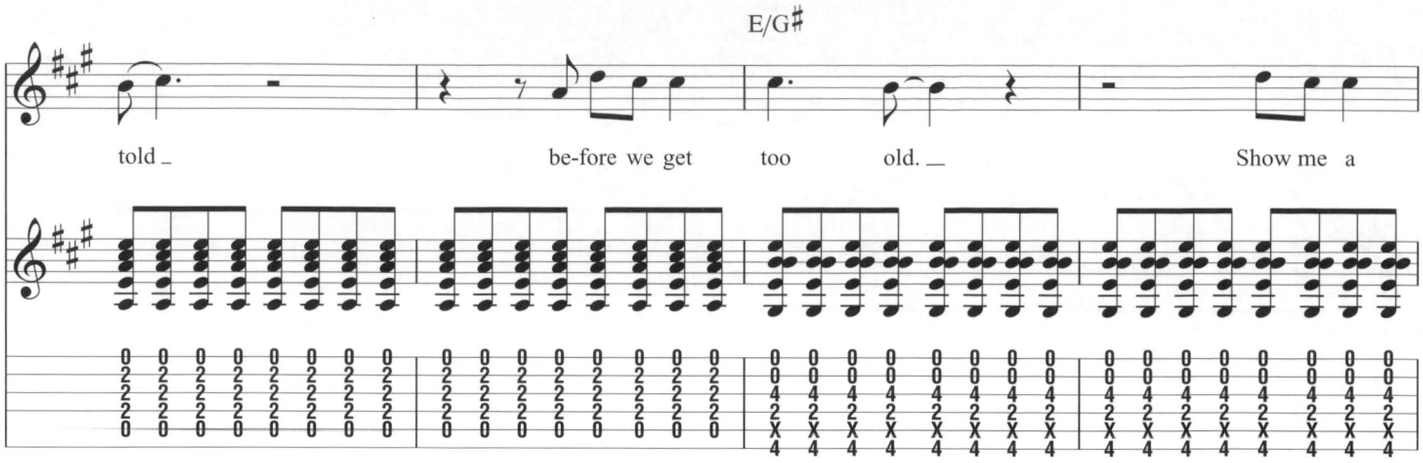

To Coda

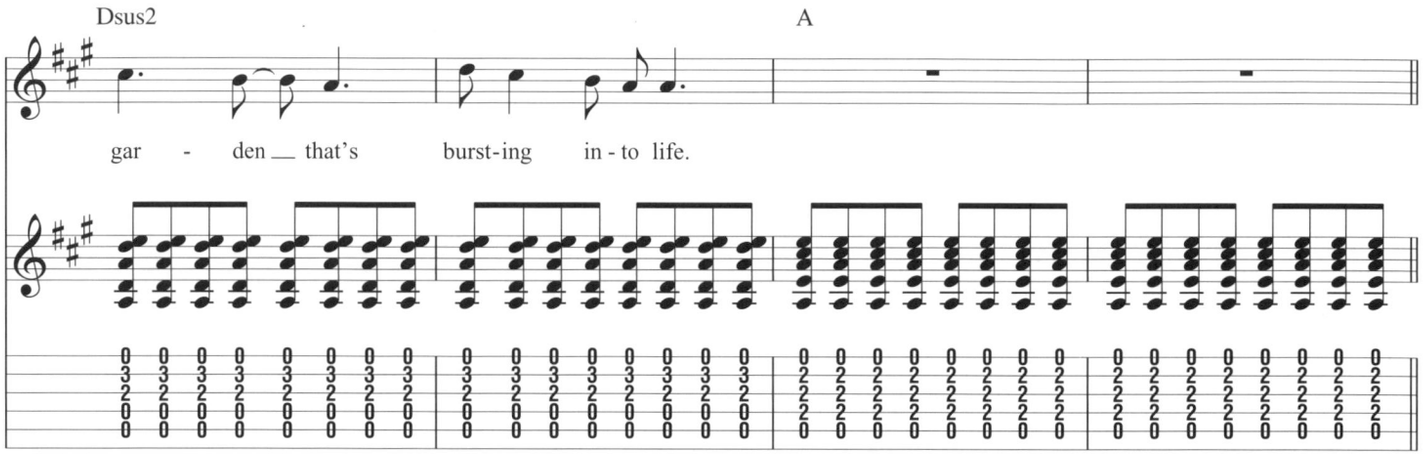

Verse

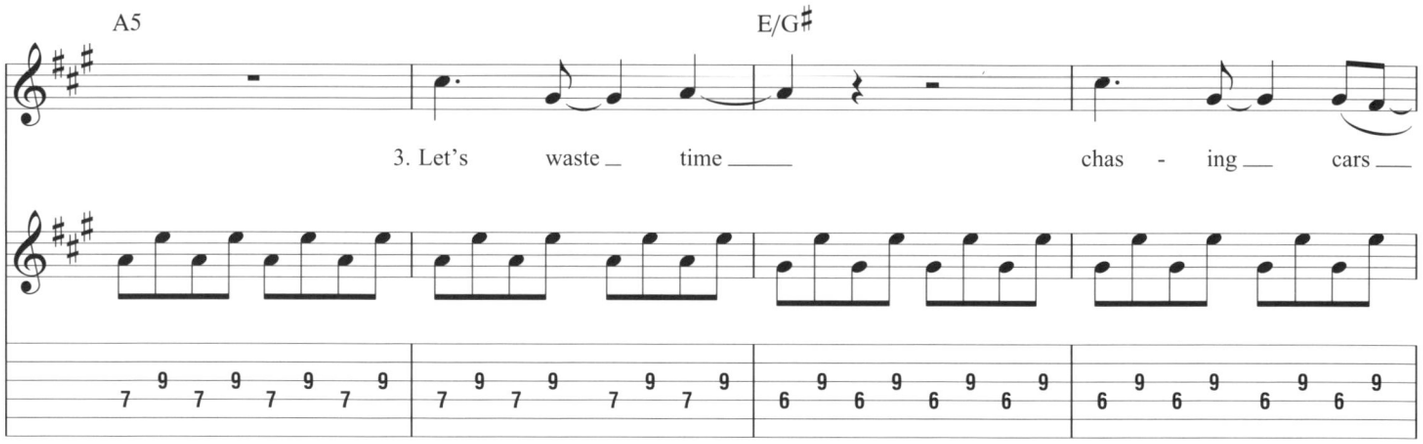

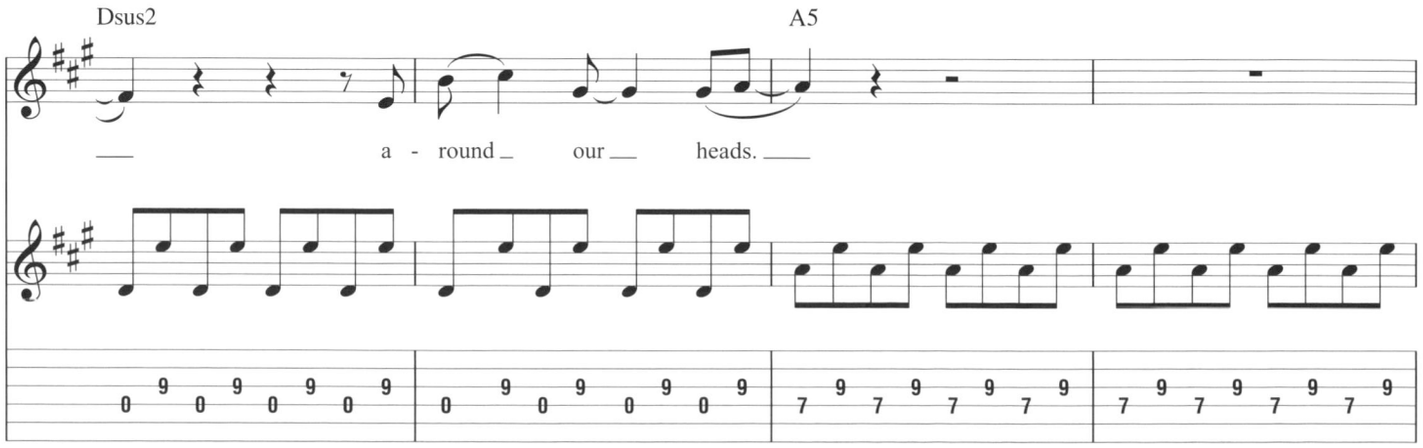

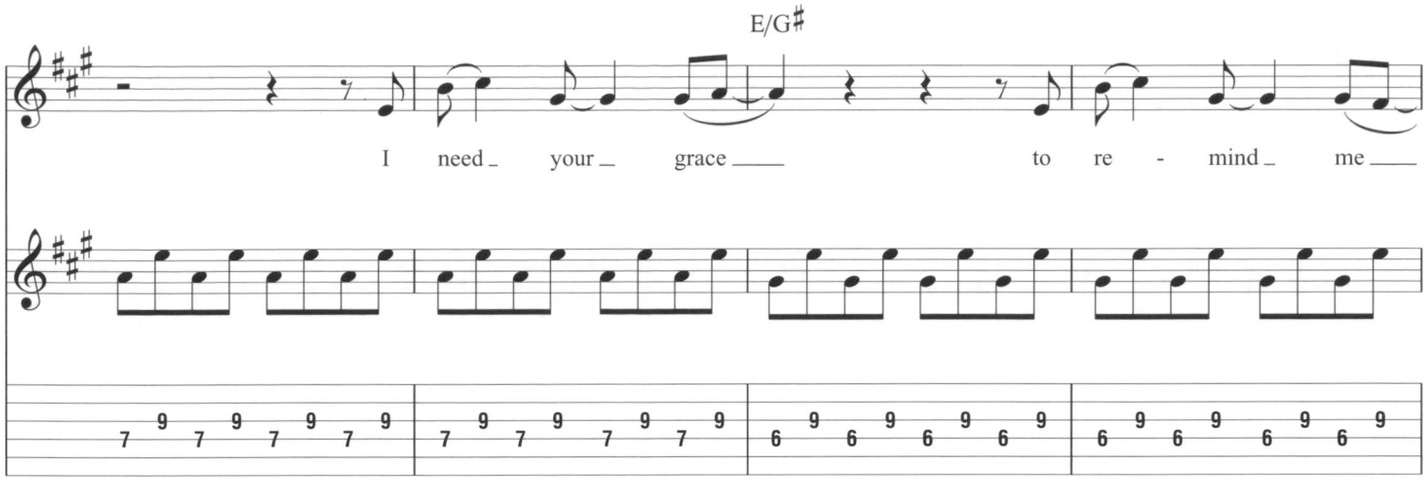

D.S. al Coda
(take 2nd ending)

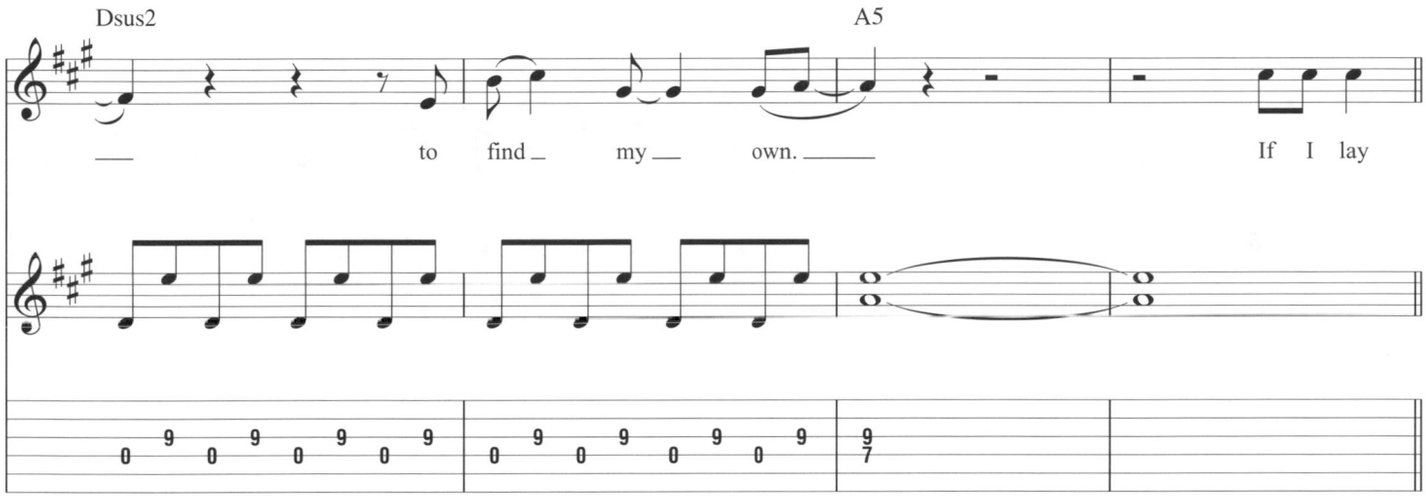

Coda

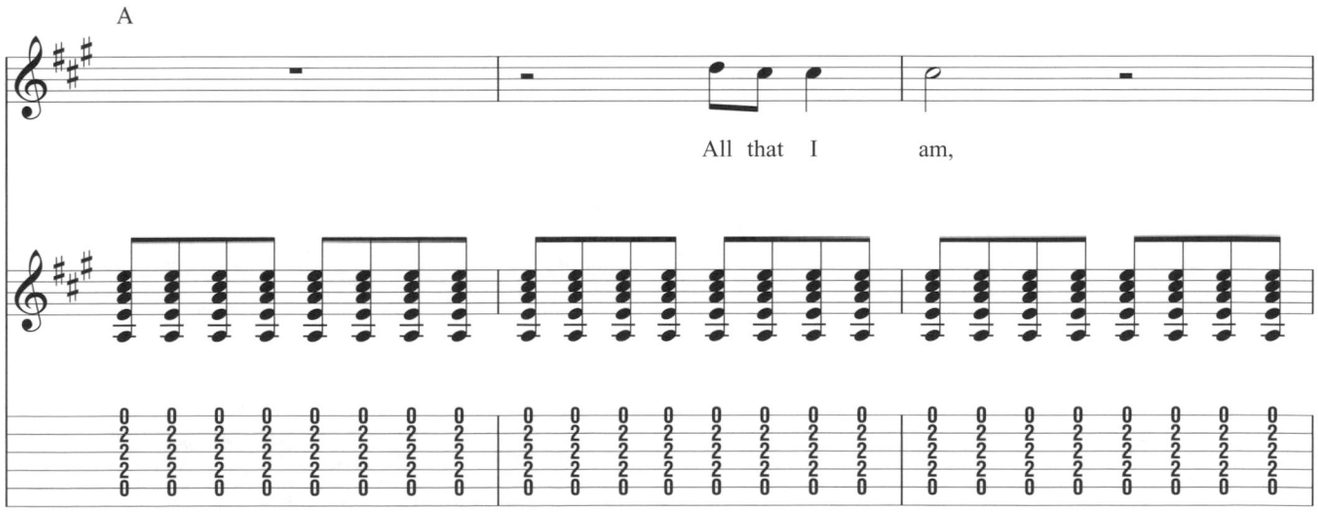

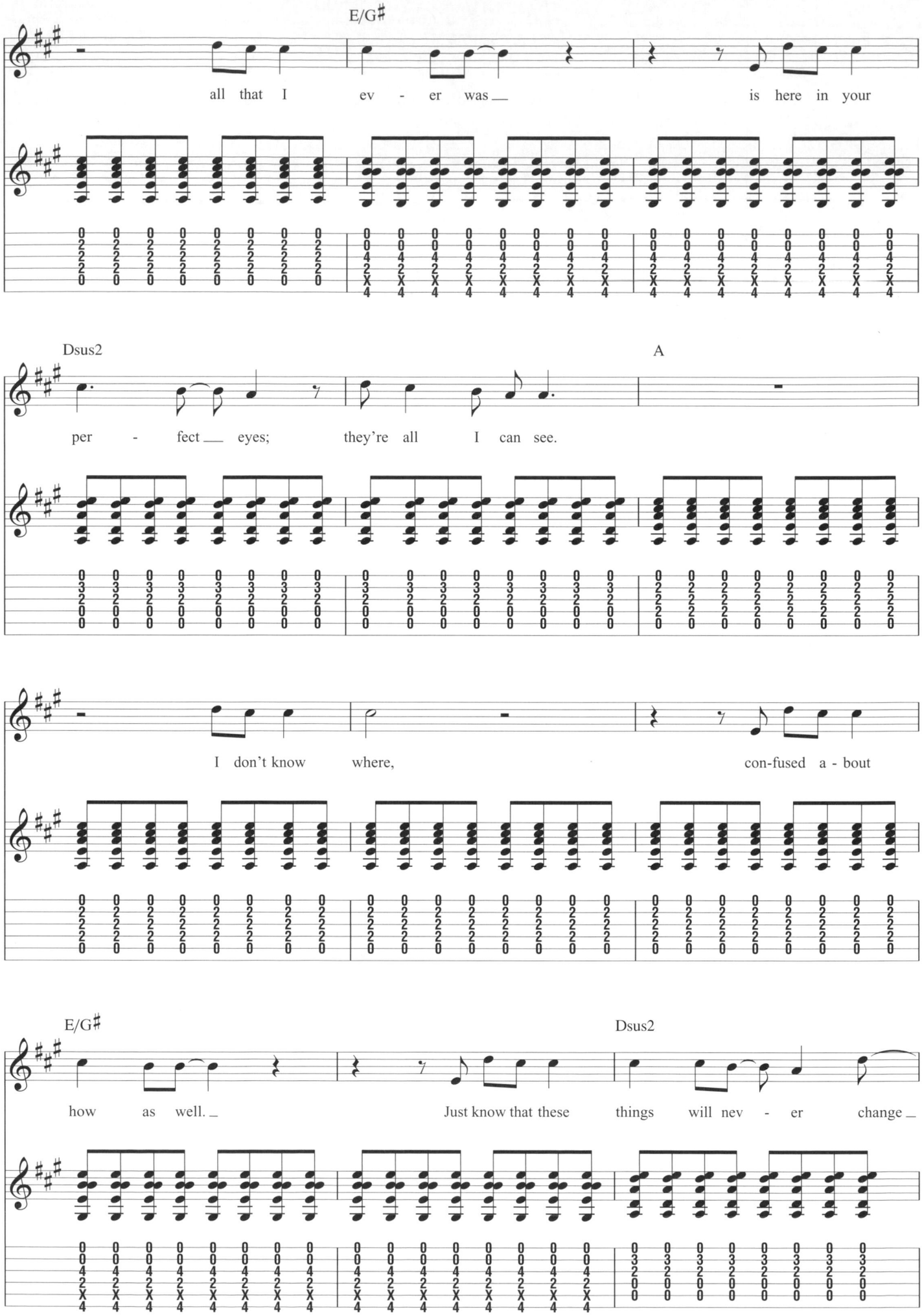
E/G♯
all that I ev - er was is here in your
Dsus2
A
per - fect eyes; they're all I can see.
I don't know where, con-fused a - bout
E/G♯
Dsus2
how as well. Just know that these things will nev - er change

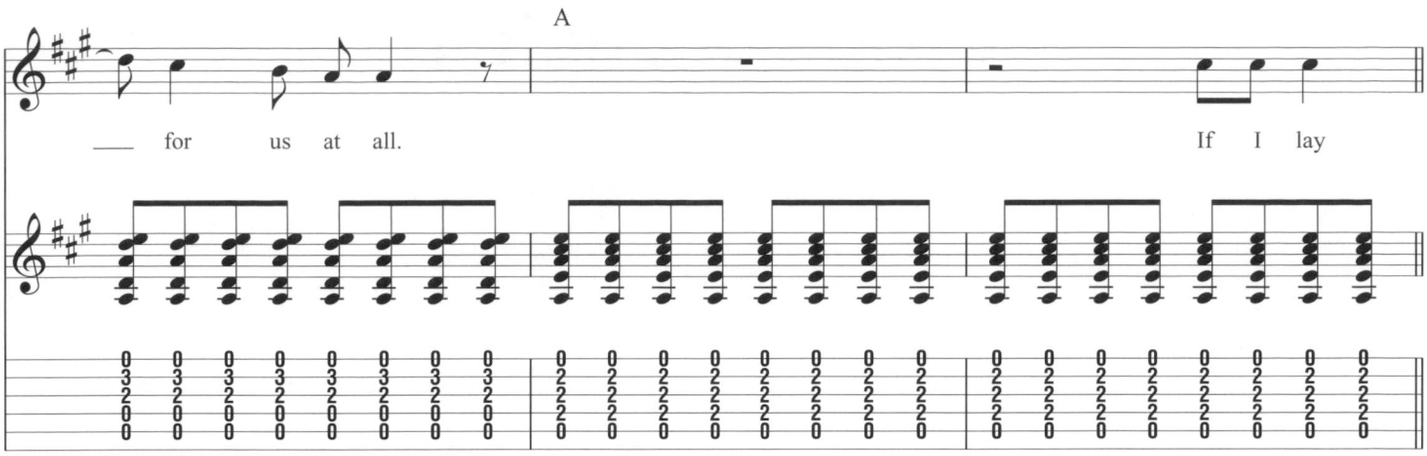

Outro

Additional Lyrics

2. I don't quite know how to say how I feel.
   Those three words are said too much. They're not enough.

Drops of Jupiter
(Tell Me)

Words and Music by Pat Monahan, James Stafford, Robert Hotchkiss, Charles Colin and Scott Underwood

Copyright © 2000 EMI April Music Inc. and Blue Lamp Music
All Rights Administered by Sony/ATV Music Publishing LLC, 424 Church Street, Suite 1200, Nashville, TN 37219
International Copyright Secured All Rights Reserved

F Fsus2 F C Csus4
she acts like sum-mer and walks like rain. Re - minds
G5 G6 Fsus2 F F6
me that there's a time to change, hey, hey, hey.
Since
C Csus4 G5 G6
the re - turn of her stay on the moon, she lis - tens like spring and she talks like June, hey,
Fsus2 F Fsus2 F
hey, hey, hey, hey, hey.
Well,

Pre-Chorus
G
D
tell me, did you sail a - cross the sun? Did you make it to the Milk - y Way
F
C
to see the lights all fad - ed, and that heav-en is o - ver - rat - ed?
G
D
Tell me, did you fall from a shoot - ing star, one with - out a per - ma - nent
Dm
F
scar, and did you miss me while you were look - in' for your - self out there?

Interlude
C
Csus4
G
G6
Fsus2
F
Fsus2
F
Fsus2
F
2. Now that
Verse
C
Csus4
G
G6
she's back from that soul va - ca - tion, trac - in' her way through the con - stel - la - tion,
Fsus2
F
Fsus2
F
Fsus2
F
hey, hey, mm. She checks

C Csus4 G G6
out Mo - zart while she does Tae - Bo. Re - minds me that there's room to grow, hey,
Fsus2 F Fsus2 F Fsus2 F
hey, hey, yeah. Now that
C Csus4 G G6
she's back in the at - mos - phere, I'm a - fraid that she might think of me as
Fsus2
plain ol' Jane. Told a sto - ry 'bout a man who was too a - fraid to fly, so he nev - er did land. But

Pre-Chorus
G
D
tell me, did the wind sweep you off your feet?
Did you fin - 'ly get the chance to dance
F
C
a - long the light of day,
and head back to the Milk - y Way?
And
G
D
tell me, did Ve - nus blow your mind?
Was it ev - 'ry - thing you want - ed to find?
Dsus2
Fsus2
and did you miss me while you were look - in' for your - self out there?

Chorus
C
G
Fsus2
Can you im - ag - ine no
C
G
love, pride, deep - fried chick-en, your best friend al - ways stick - in'
Fsus2
up for you
e - ven when I know you're wrong? Can you im - ag - ine no

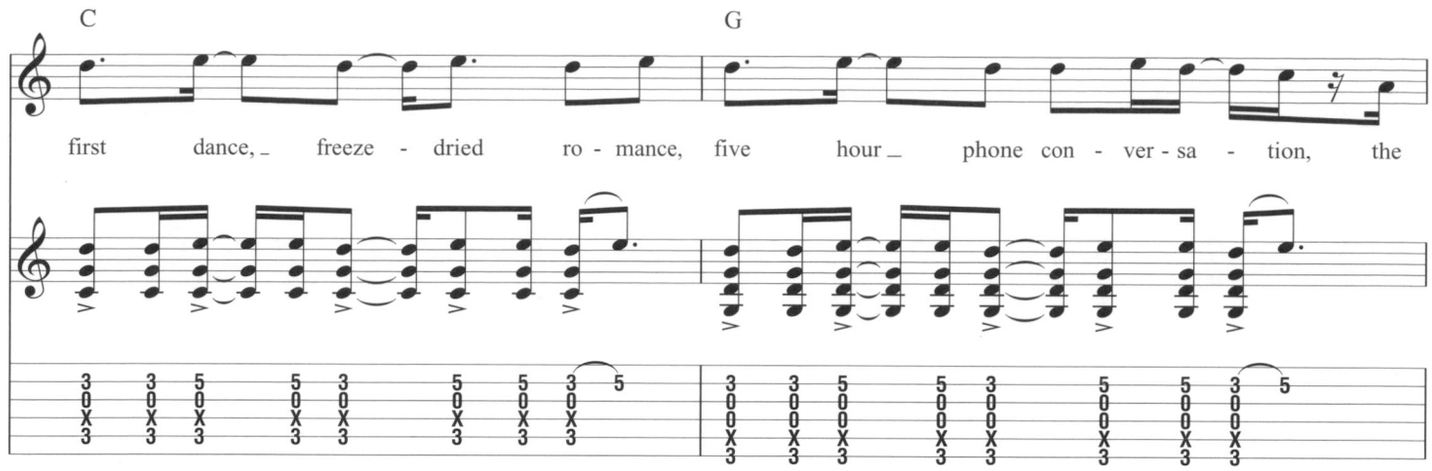
C
G
first dance, freeze - dried ro - mance, five hour phone con - ver - sa - tion, the

B♭
C/B♭
B♭
F
best soy lat - te that you ev - er had and me? But

Pre-Chorus

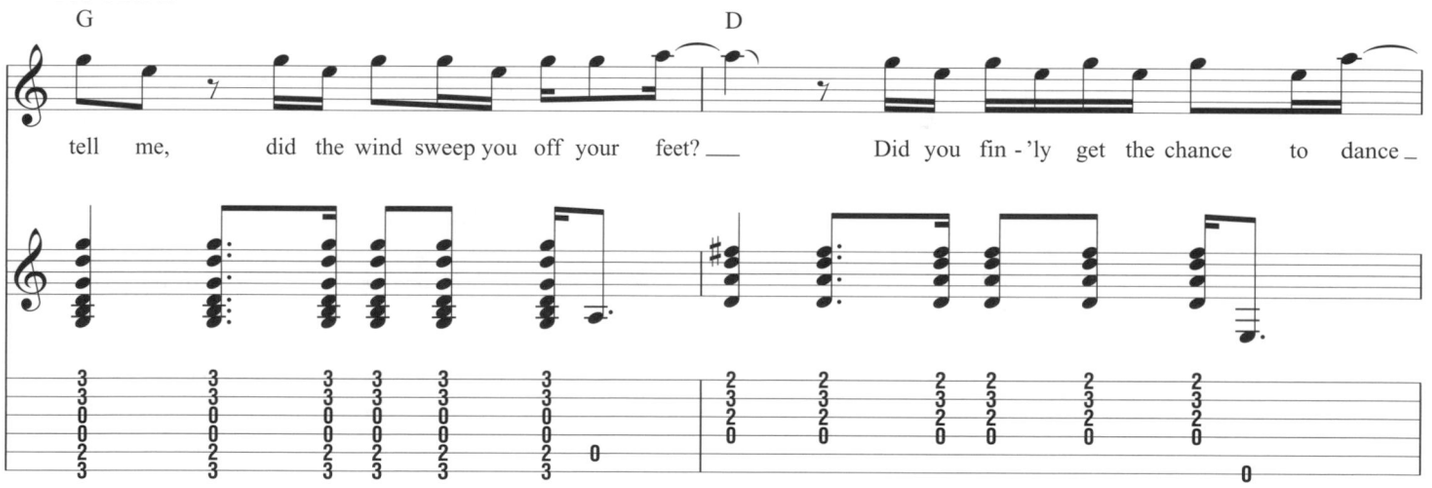
G
D
tell me, did the wind sweep you off your feet? Did you fin - 'ly get the chance to dance

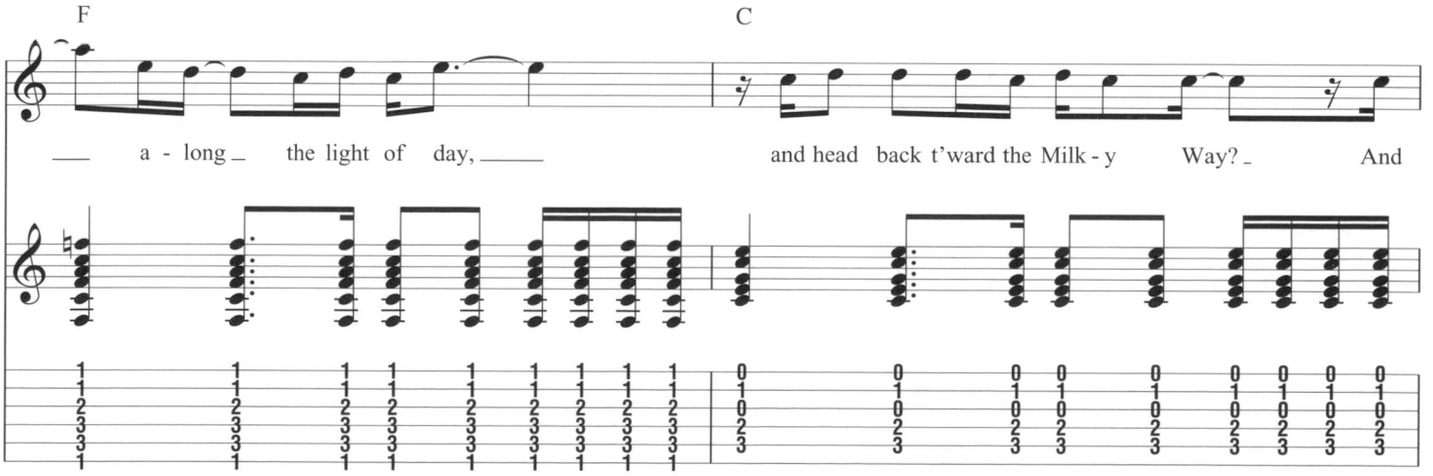
F
C
a - long the light of day, and head back t'ward the Milk - y Way? And

G
D
tell me, did you sail a - cross the sun? Did you make it to the Milk - y Way
Fsus2
C
to see the lights all fad - ed, and that heav-en is o - ver - rat - ed? And
G
D
tell me, did you fall from a shoot-ing star, one with - out a per - ma - nent
Dsus2
Fsus2
N.C.
scar, and did you miss me while you were look - in' for your - self?

Outro-Chorus
C
G
(Na, na, na, na, na, na, na, na, na, na, na, na, na, na,
Fsus2
And did you fin-'ly get the chance to dance a-long the light of day?
na, na.
C
G
Na, na, na, na, na, na, na, na, na, na, na, na, na, na,
And did you

Fsus2
fall from a shoot-ing star,
fall from a shoot-ing star?
na, na.
C
G
Na, na, na, na, na, na, na, na, na, na, na, na,
And are you
B♭
C/B♭
B♭
F
lone - ly look - in' for your - self out there?
na, na.)

Hey Jude

Words and Music by John Lennon and Paul McCartney

*Symbols in parentheses represent chord names respective to capoed guitar.
Symbols above reflect actual sounding chords. Capoed fret is "0" in tab.

Copyright © 1968 Sony/ATV Music Publishing LLC
Copyright Renewed
All Rights Administered by Sony/ATV Music Publishing LLC, 424 Church Street, Suite 1200, Nashville, TN 37219
International Copyright Secured All Rights Reserved

F
(E)
B♭
(A)
get her. The min - ute you let her un - der your

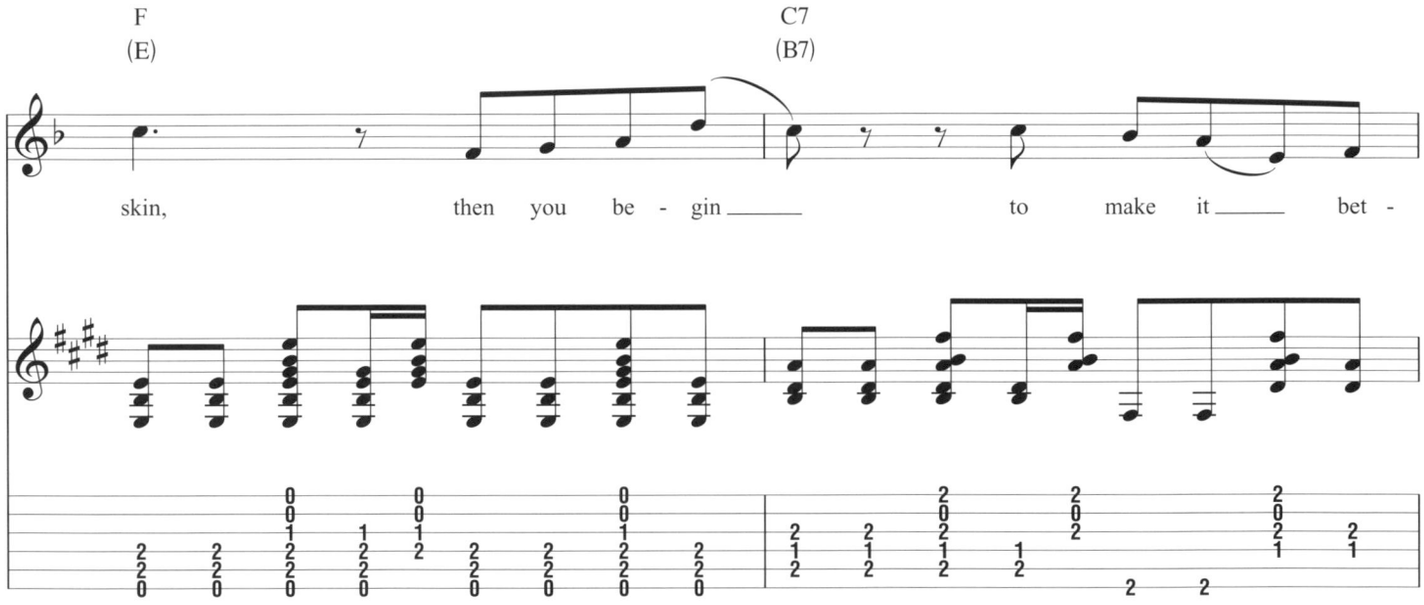
F
(E)
C7
(B7)
skin, then you be - gin to make it bet -

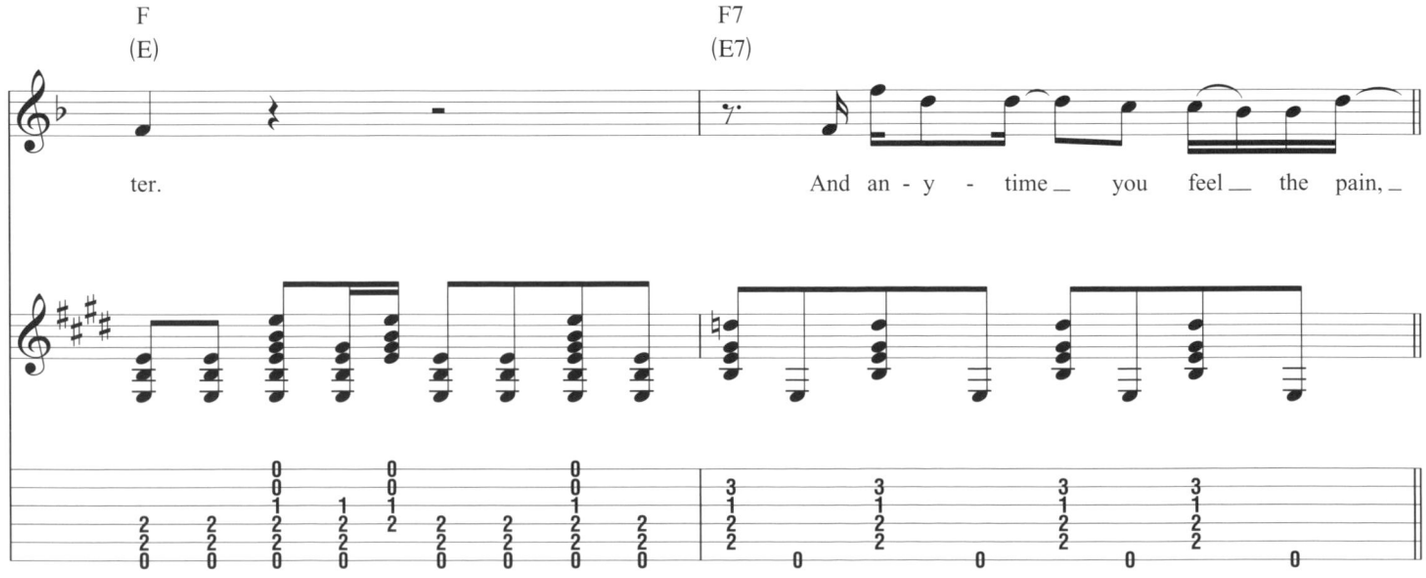
F
(E)
F7
(E7)
ter. And an - y - time you feel the pain,

Bridge
B♭ (A)
B♭/A (A/G♯)
Gm7 (F♯m7)
B♭/F (A/E)
hey, Jude, re - frain. Don't car - ry the world
See additional lyrics
C7 (B7)
F (E)
up - on your shoul - der.
F7 (E7)
B♭ (A)
B♭/A (A/G♯)
For well you know that it's a fool who plays it cool

Gm7
(F♯m7)
B♭/F
(A/E)
C7
(B7)
F
(E)
by mak - ing his world a lit - tle cold - er.
Na, na, na,

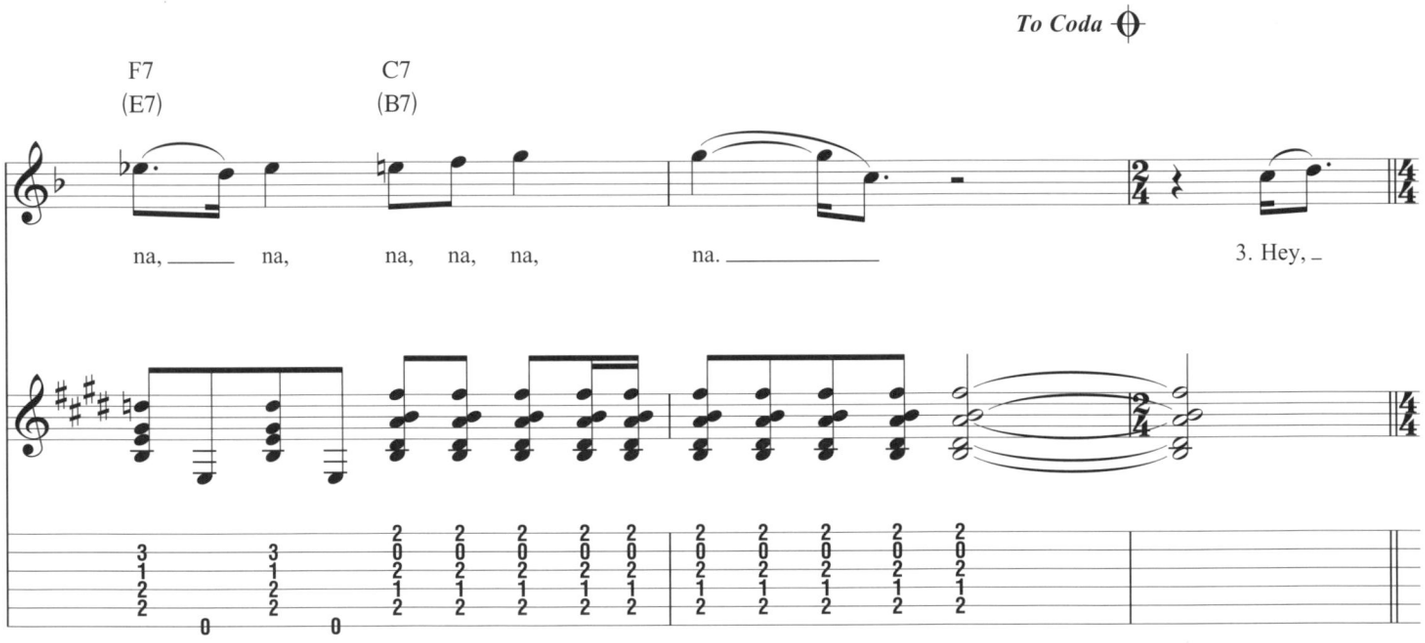
To Coda
F7
(E7)
C7
(B7)
na, na, na, na, na, na.
3. Hey,

Verse
F
(E)
C7
(B7)
Jude, don't let me down.
You have found her; now go and

F
(E)
B♭
(A)
get her.
Re - mem - ber to let her in - to your
(So let it out and let it in.
Hey, Jude.)

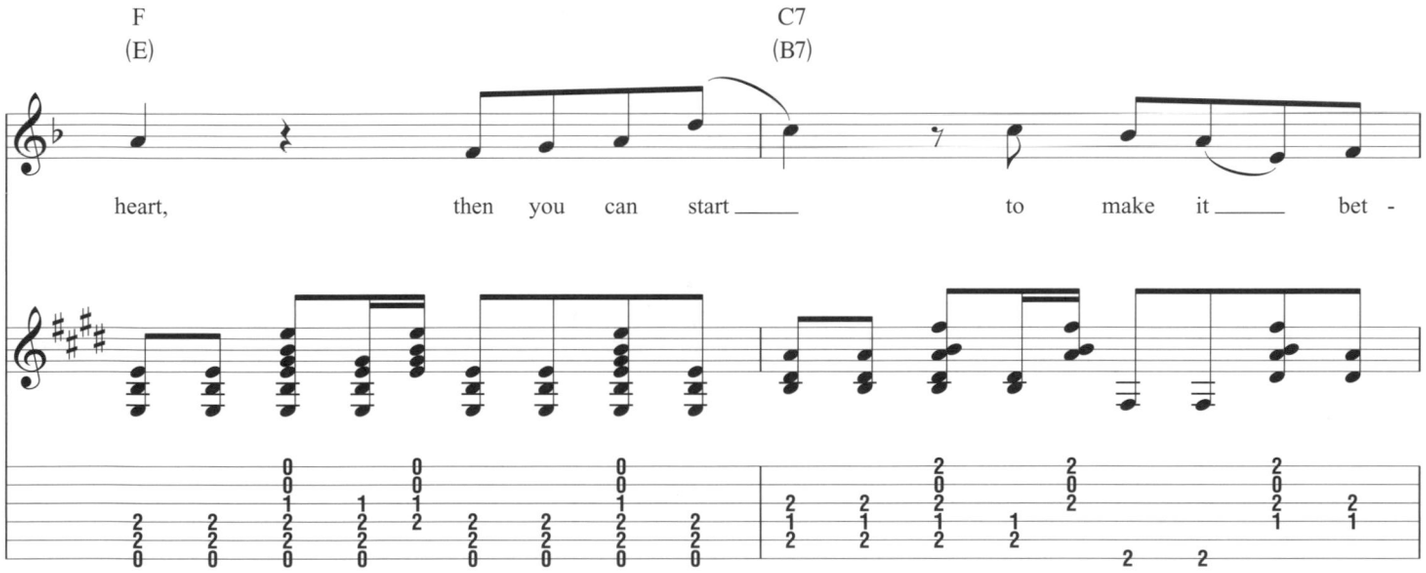
F
(E)
C7
(B7)
heart, then you can start
to make it bet -

D.S. al Coda

F
(E)
F7
(E7)
ter.
So let it out and let it in.

Coda
Verse
F
(E)
C7
(B7)
4. Hey, Jude, don't make it bad. Take a
F
(E)
B♭
(A)
sad song and make it bet - ter. Re - mem-ber to let her un - der your
F
(E)
C7
(B7)
skin. Then you be - gin to make it bet -

Additional Lyrics

Bridge So let it out and let it in.
Hey, Jude, begin.
You're waiting for someone to perform with.
And don't you know that it's just you?
Hey, Jude, you'll do.
The movement you need is on your shoulder.
Na, na, na, na, na, na, na, na, na.

Half of My Heart

Words and Music by John Mayer

Copyright © 2009 Sony/ATV Music Publishing LLC and Specific Harm Music
All Rights Administered by Sony/ATV Music Publishing LLC, 424 Church Street, Suite 1200, Nashville, TN 37219
International Copyright Secured All Rights Reserved

B♭sus2 (Asus2)
F (E)
C5 (B5)
___ friends;
free to roam, ___ made a home _
Dm7 (C♯m7)
B♭sus2 (Asus2)
F (E)
C5 (B5)
_____ out of ev - 'ry-where I've ___ been.
Then _
Pre-Chorus
B♭sus2 (Asus2)
F (E)
___ you come crash - ing ___ in _____
like the real -
See additional lyrics
C5 (B5)
Dm7 (C♯m7)
B♭sus2 (Asus2)
- est thing. _____
Try'n' _ my best to un - der - stand _

F
(E)
C5
(B5)
all that your love can bring. Oh,
Chorus
B♭sus2
(Asus2)
F
(E)
C5
(B5)
Dm7
(C♯m7)
B♭sus2
(Asus2)
F
(E)
C5
(B5)
half of my heart's got a grip on the sit - u - a - tion, half of my heart takes time.
B♭sus2
(Asus2)
F
(E)
C5
(B5)
Dm7
(C♯m7)
Half of my heart's got a right mind to tell you that I
B♭sus2
(Asus2)
C5
(B5)
can't keep lov - ing you,
(Can't keep lov - ing you.)
oh, with half of my heart.

1.
F (E)
C5 (B5)
Dm7 (C♯m7)
B♭sus2 (Asus2)
F (E)
C5 (B5)
Dm7 (C♯m7)
B♭sus2 (Asus2)
2.
F (E)
C5 (B5)
Dm7 (C♯m7)
B♭sus2 (Asus2)
F (E)
C5 (B5)
Dm7 (C♯m7)
B♭sus2 (Asus2)
With half of my heart.
Your faith
Bridge
F (E)
Am7 (G♯m7)
Cm7 (Bm7)
C7sus2 (B7sus2)
is strong
but I can on - ly fall short for so
Gm7 (F♯m7)
F (E)
Am7 (G♯m7)
long.
Down the road,
lat - er on,
you will

Cm7
(Bm7)
C7sus2
(B7sus2)
Gm7
(F♯m7)
B♭sus2
(Asus2)
hate that I nev - er gave more to you — than — half of my heart, —

C/E
(B/D♯)
but I can't stop — lov - ing you.
(I can't stop lov - ing you.
I

B♭sus2
(Asus2)
C/E
(B/D♯)
can't stop — lov - ing you.
I can't stop lov - ing you.)
I can't stop — lov - ing you —

Outro-Chorus
N.C.
B♭sus2 (Asus2)
F (E)
C5 (B5)
Dm7 (C♯m7)
with half of my, half of my heart, oh,
half of my heart.
Half of my heart's got a real
good i - mag - i - na - tion, half of my heart's got you.
Half of my heart's got a right mind to tell you that half of my heart won't do.

B♭sus2 (Asus2) F (E) C5 (B5) Dm7 (C♯m7)
Half of my heart is a shot - gun wed-ding to a bride
B♭sus2 (Asus2) F (E) C5 (B5) B♭sus2 (Asus2) F (E) C5 (B5)
with a pa - per ring. And half of my heart is the heart
Dm7 (C♯m7) B♭sus2 (Asus2) F (E) C5 (B5)
of a man who's nev - er tru - ly loved an - y - thing.
B♭sus2 (Asus2) F (E) C5 (B5) Dm7 (C♯m7) B♭sus2 (Asus2) F (E) C5 (B5)
Half of my heart, oh, half of my heart.

Additional Lyrics

2. I was made to believe I'd never love somebody else.
Made a plan, stay the man who can only love himself.

Pre-Chorus Lonely was the song I sang till the day you came.
Showing me another way, and all that my love can bring.

A Horse with No Name

Words and Music by Dewey Bunnell

© 1972 (Renewed) WARNER/CHAPPELL MUSIC LTD.
All Rights for the Western Hemisphere Controlled by WB MUSIC CORP.
All Rights Reserved Used by Permission

D6/F♯
Em
D6/F♯
and things. There was sand and hills and rains. The
Em9
D6/F♯
first thing I met was a fly with a buzz and the
Em9
D6/F♯
Em9
sky with no clouds. The heat was hot and the
D6/F♯
Em9
D6/F♯
ground was dry, but the air was full of sounds. I've

Chorus
Em9
D6/F♯
been through the des - ert on a horse with no name. It felt good to be out of the
rain. In the des - ert you can re - mem - ber your name be - cause there
ain't no one for to give you no pain. La, la, la,
la, la, la, la, la, la, la, la.

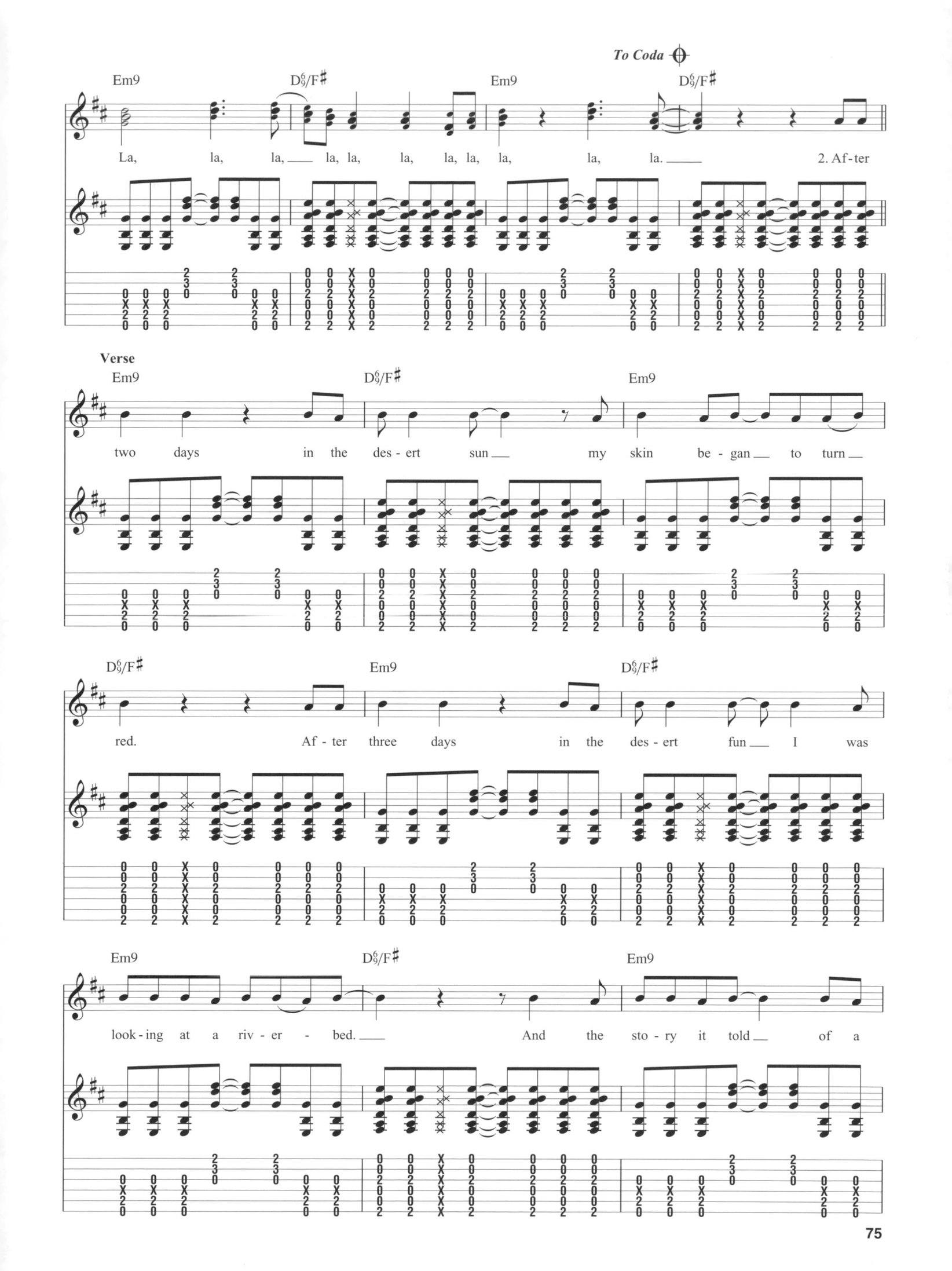
To Coda
Em9
D6/F♯
Em9
D6/F♯
La, la, la, la, la, la, la, la, la, la, la. 2. Af-ter
Verse
Em9
D6/F♯
Em9
two days in the des - ert sun my skin be - gan to turn
D6/F♯
Em9
D6/F♯
red. Af - ter three days in the des - ert fun I was
Em9
D6/F♯
Em9
look - ing at a riv - er - bed. And the sto - ry it told of a

D6/F♯
Em9
D6/F♯
riv - er that flowed, made me sad to think it was dead. You see, I've
Chorus
Em9
D6/F♯
Em9
been through the des - ert on a horse with no name. It felt good to be out of the
D6/F♯
Em9
D6/F♯
rain. In the des - ert you can re - mem - ber your name 'cause there
Em9
D6/F♯
Em9
ain't no one for to give you no pain. La, la, la, la,

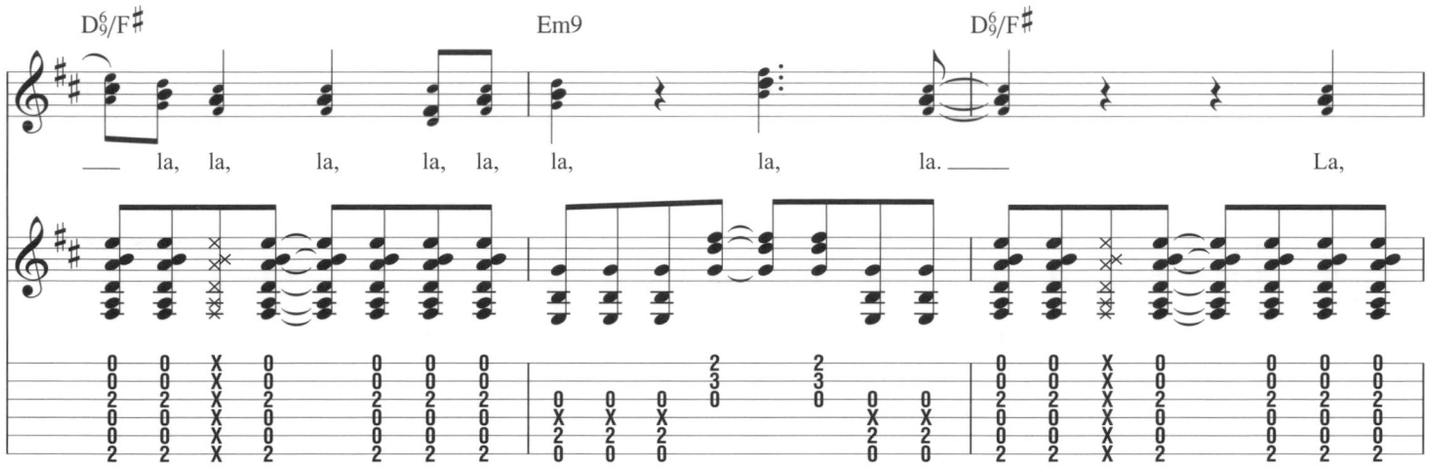
D6/F♯
Em9
D6/F♯
la, la, la, la, la, la, la, la. La,

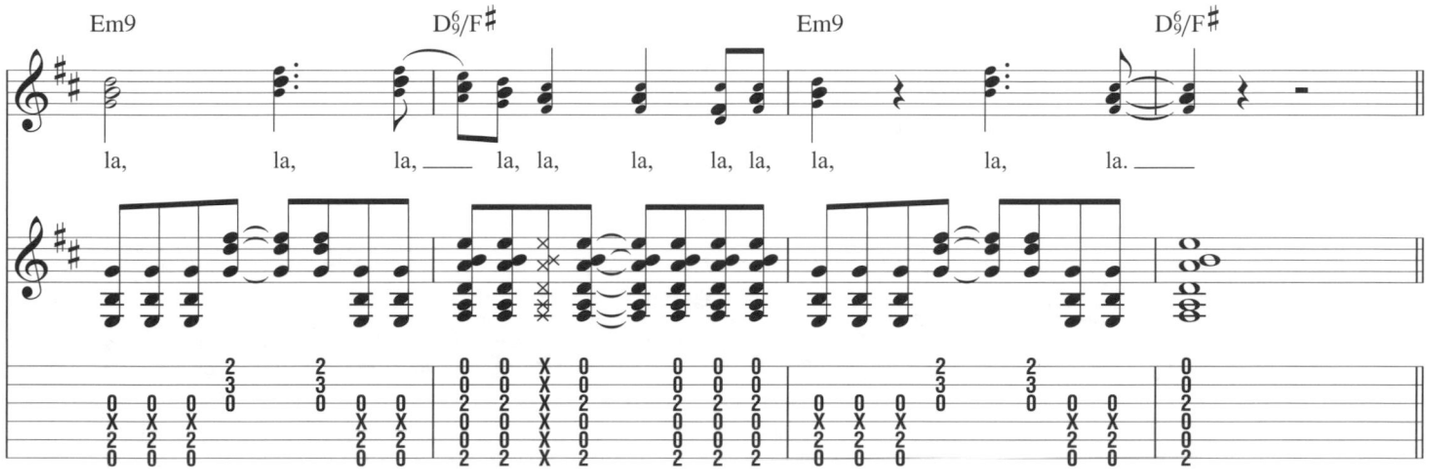
Em9
D6/F♯
Em9
D6/F♯
la, la, la, la, la, la, la, la, la, la, la.

Guitar Solo

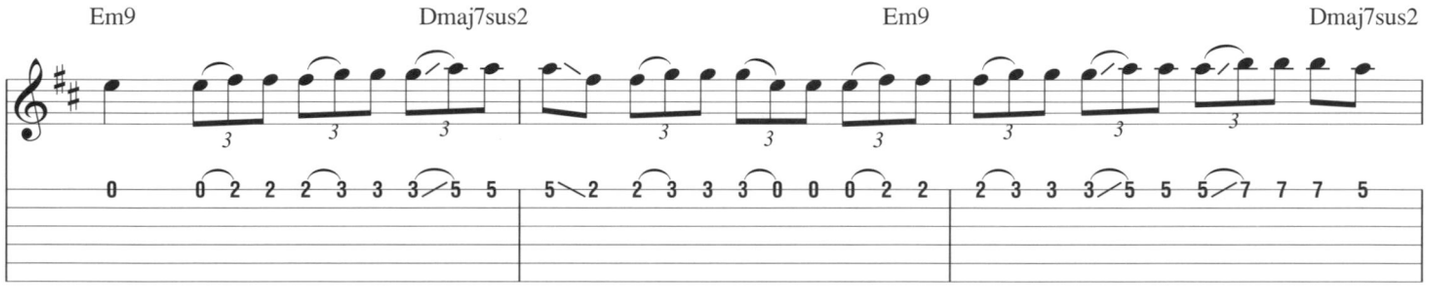
Em9
Dmaj7sus2
Em9
Dmaj7sus2

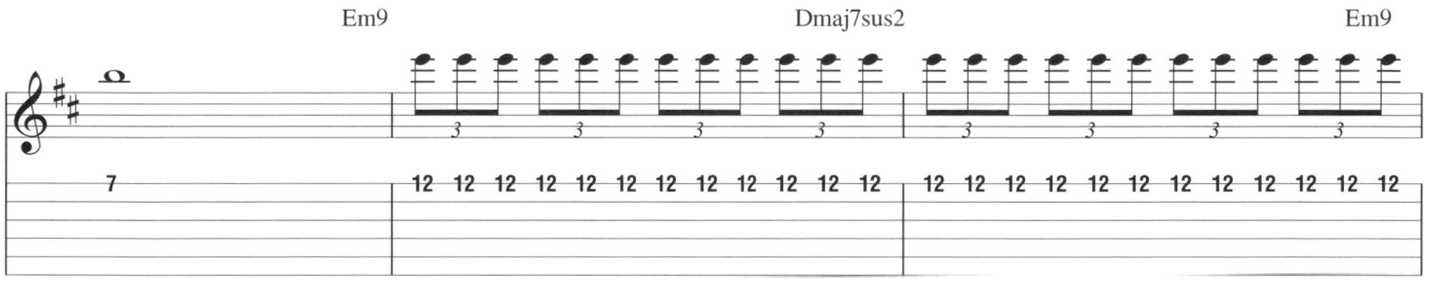
Em9
Dmaj7sus2
Em9

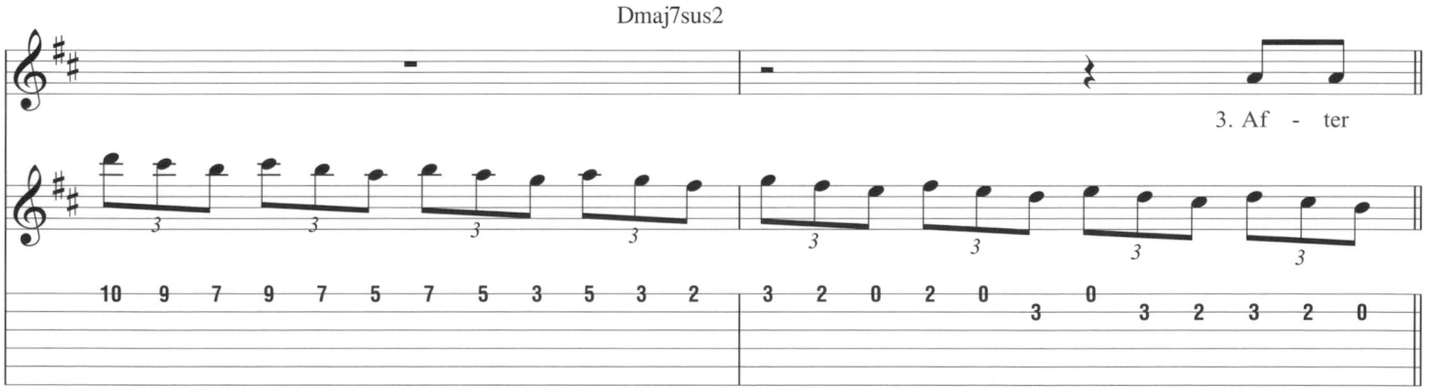
Dmaj7sus2
3. Af - ter

Verse
Em9
D6/F♯
Em9
nine days I let the horse run free 'cause the des - ert had turned to sea.
D6/F♯
Em9
D6/F♯
There were plants and birds and rocks and things. There was
Em
D6/F♯
Em9
sand and hills and rains. The o - cean is a des - ert with a
D6/F♯
Em9
D6/F♯
life un - der - ground and the per - fect dis - guise a - bove. Un - der the

Em9
D6/F♯
Em9
cit - ies lies a heart made of ground, but the hu - mans will give no love.
D.S. al Coda
Coda
D6/F♯
You see I've
D6/F♯
Outro
Em9
La, la, La, la, la,
D6/F♯
Em9
D6/F♯
la, la, la, la, la, la, la, la. La,
Play 3 times & fade
Em9
D6/F♯
Em9
D6/F♯
la, la, la, la, la, la, la, la, la, la, la.

Island in the Sun

Words and Music by Rivers Cuomo

Copyright © 2001 E.O. Smith Music
International Copyright Secured All Rights Reserved

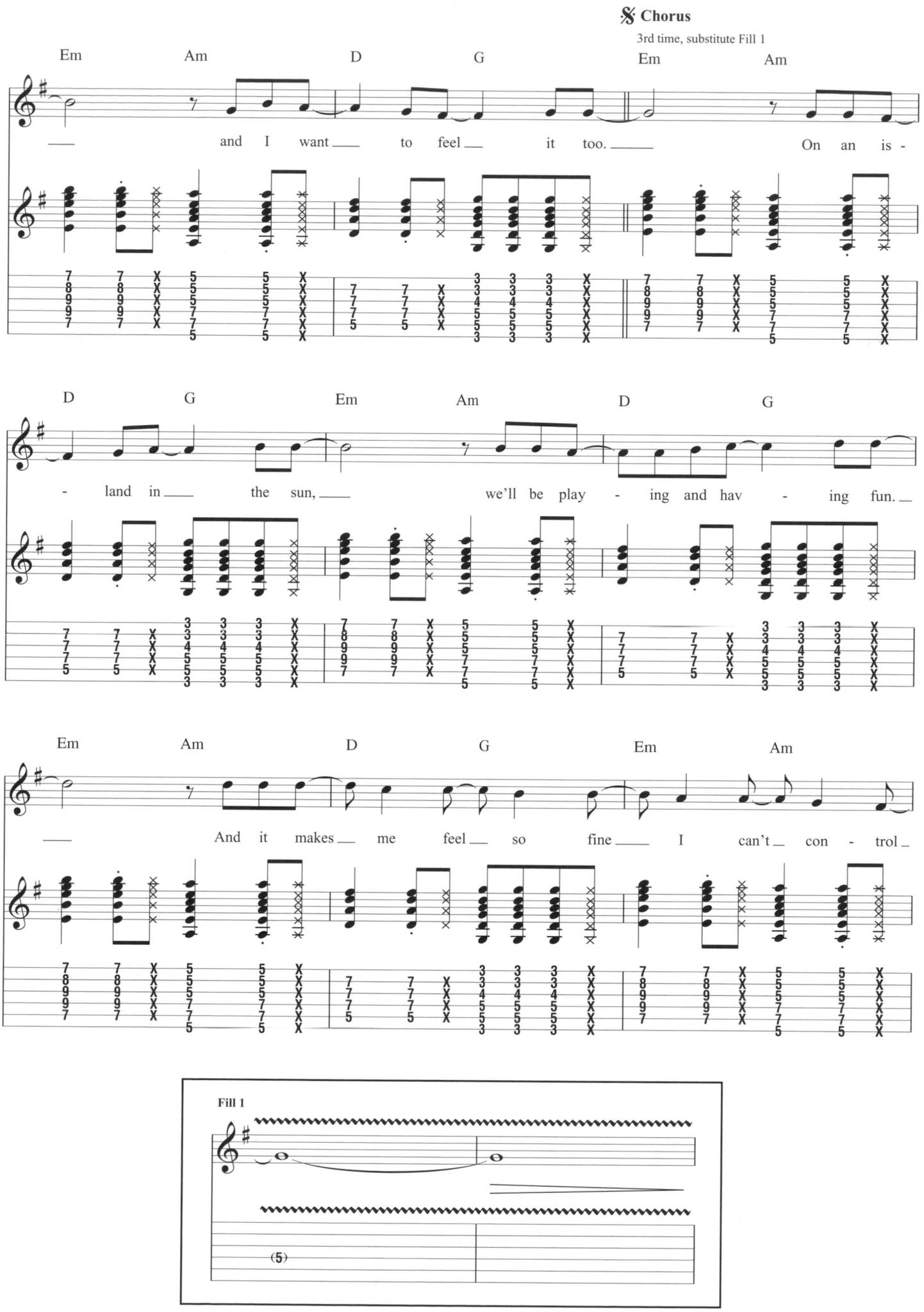
Chorus
3rd time, substitute Fill 1
Em Am D G Em Am
and I want to feel it too. On an is -
D G Em Am D G
- land in the sun, we'll be play - ing and hav - ing fun.
Em Am D G Em Am
And it makes me feel so fine I can't con - trol
Fill 1
(5)

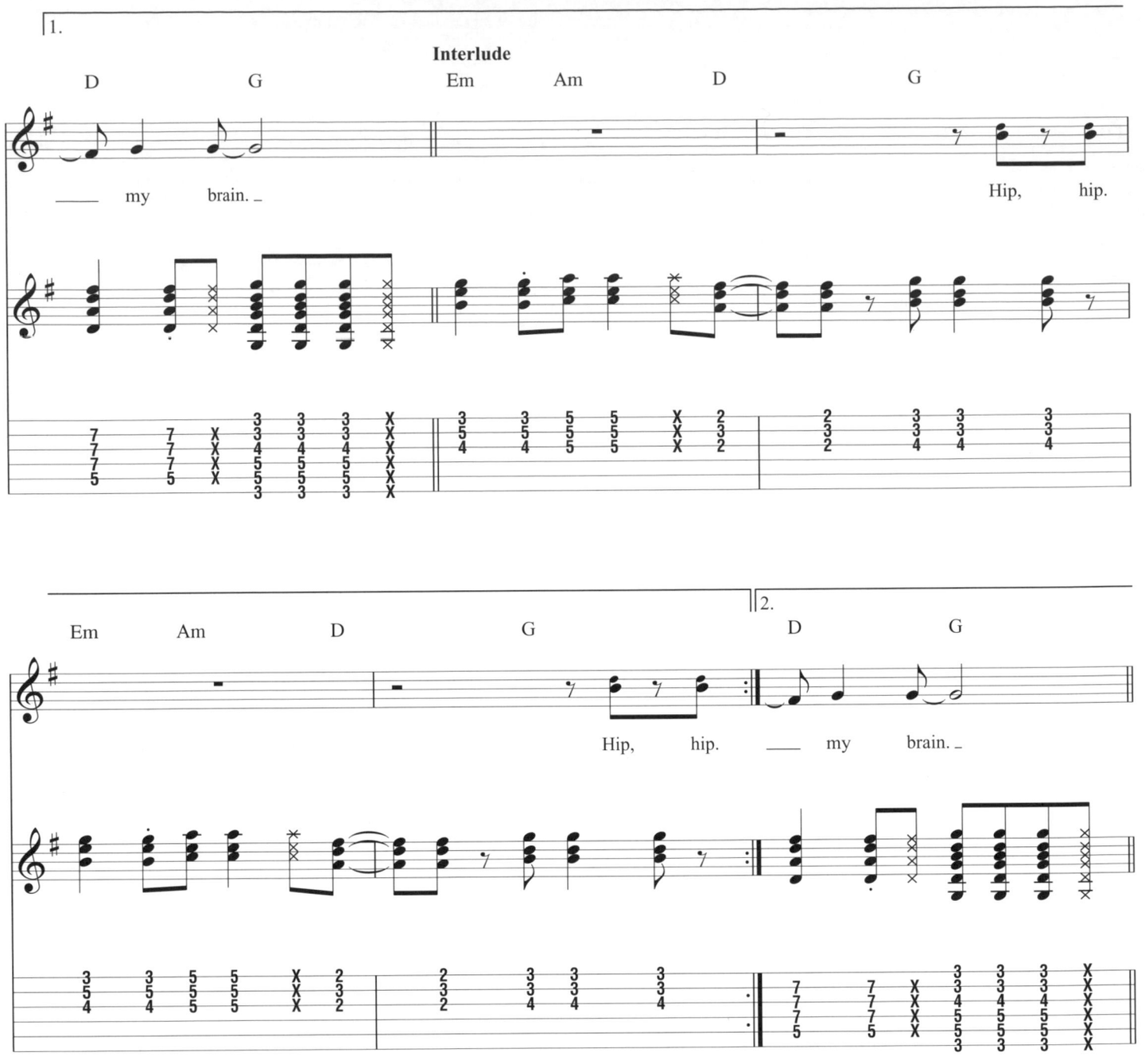
1.
Interlude
D G Em Am D G
my brain.
Hip, hip.
Em Am D G
Hip, hip. my brain.
2.
D G

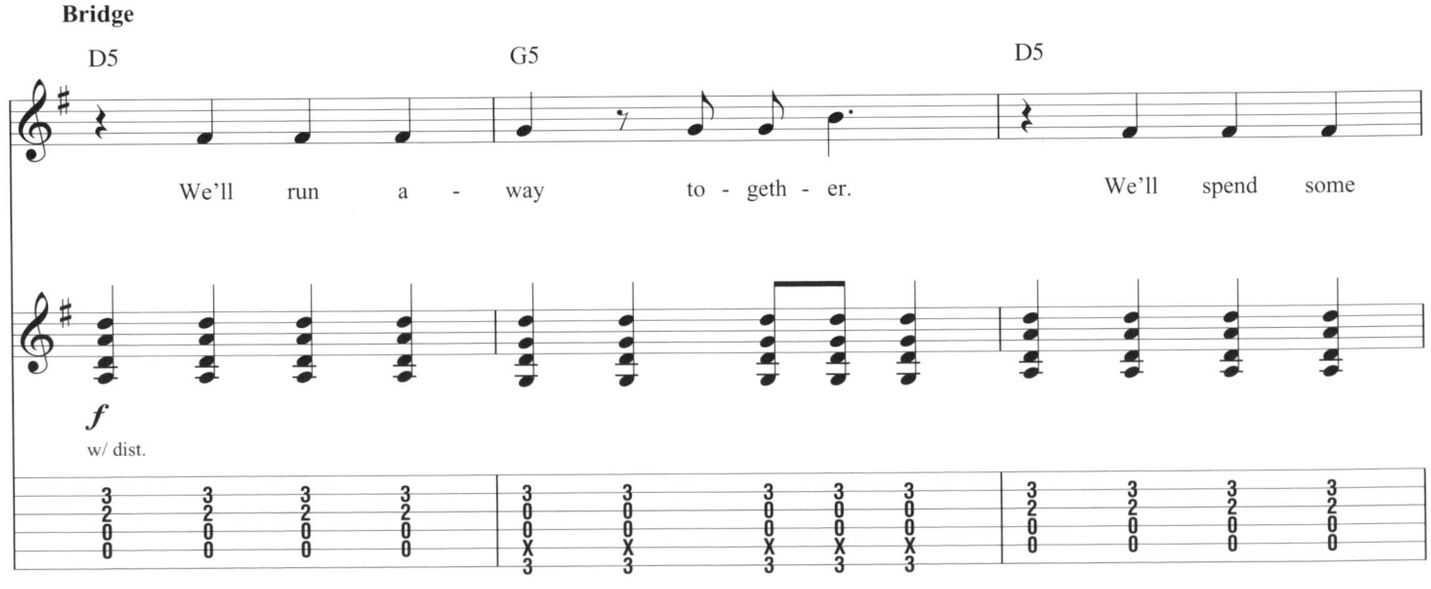
Bridge
D5 G5 D5
We'll run a - way to - geth - er. We'll spend some
f
w/ dist.

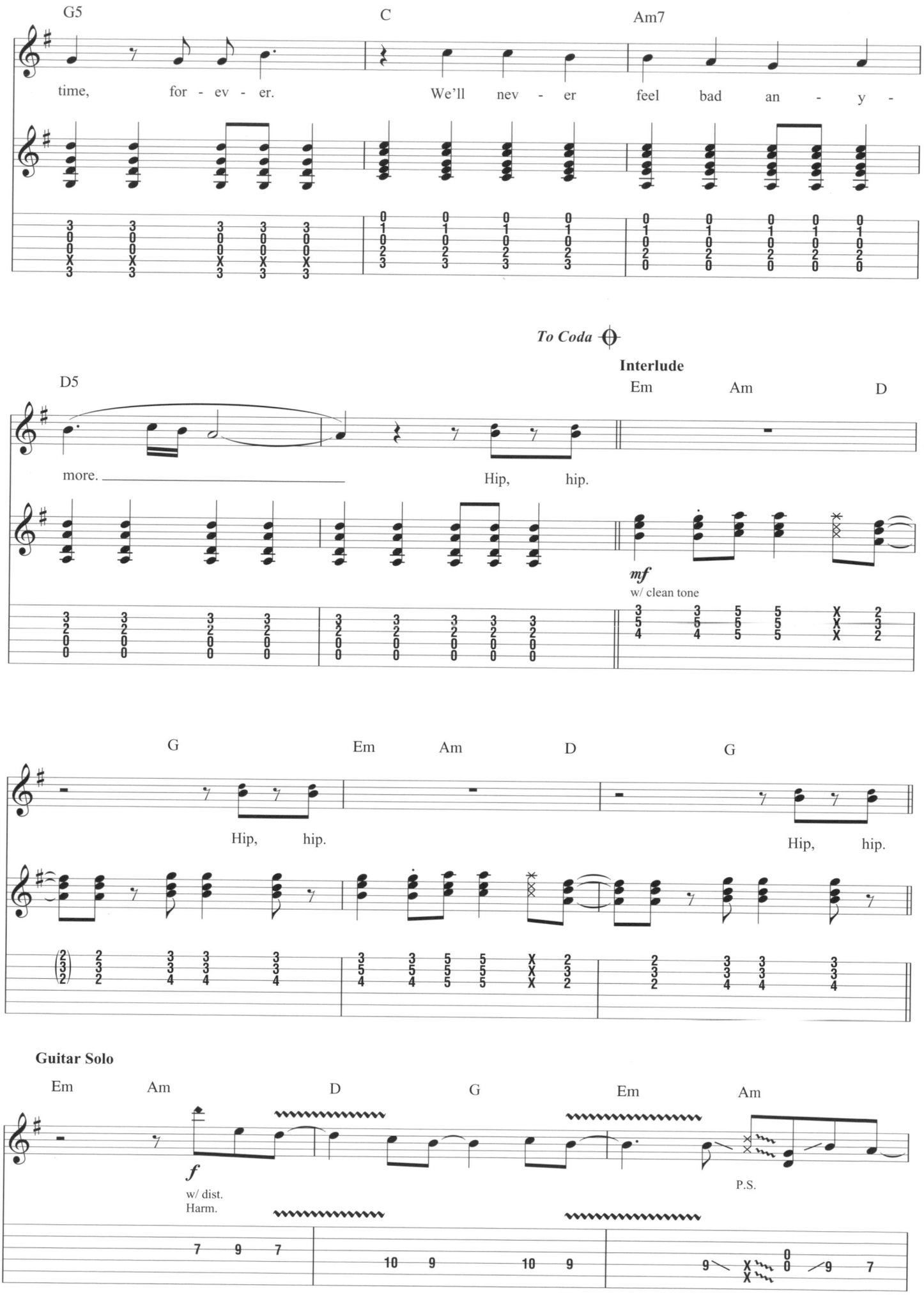
G5
C
Am7
time, for - ev - er.
We'll nev - er feel bad an - y -
To Coda
Interlude
D5
Em
Am
D
more.
Hip, hip.
mf
w/ clean tone
G
Em
Am
D
G
Hip, hip.
Hip, hip.
Guitar Solo
Em
Am
D
G
Em
Am
f
w/ dist.
Harm.
P.S.

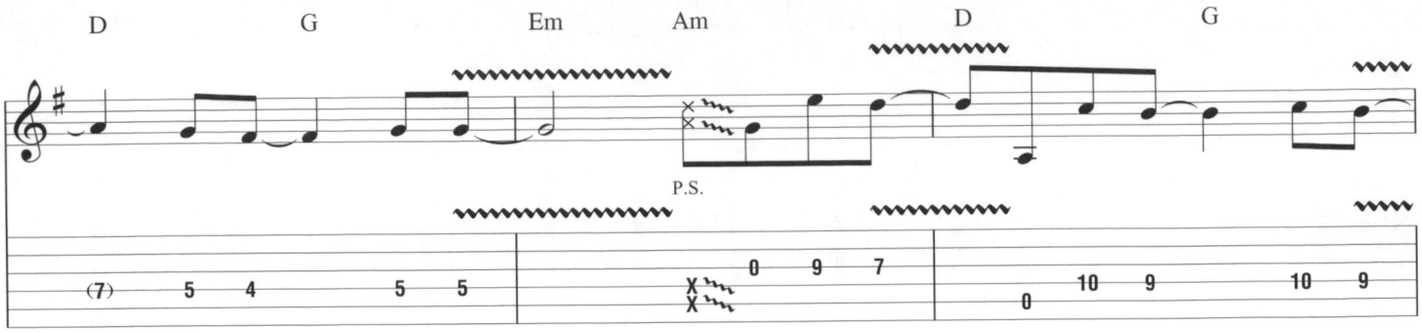

D.S. al Coda
(take 2nd ending)

Coda

Outro

Repeat and fade

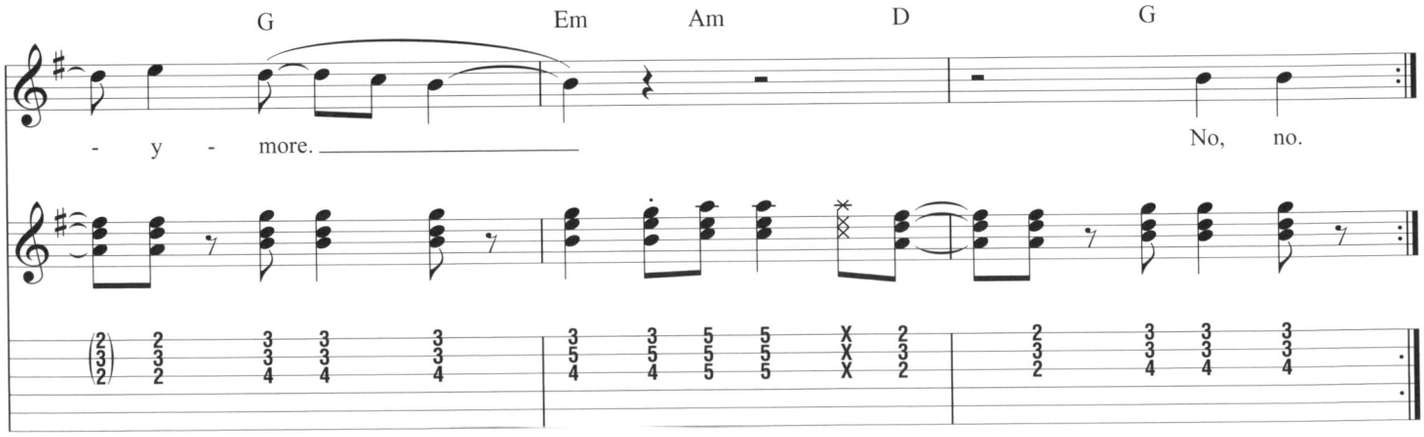

Additional Lyrics

2. When you're on a golden sea,
   You don't need no memory,
   Just a place to call your own
   As we drift into the zone.

One

Lyrics by Bono and The Edge
Music by U2

Copyright © 1991 UNIVERSAL - POLYGRAM INTERNATIONAL MUSIC PUBLISHING B.V.
All Rights in the United States and Canada Controlled and Administered by UNIVERSAL - POLYGRAM INTERNATIONAL PUBLISHING, INC.
All Rights Reserved Used by Permission

Fmaj7
G
or do you feel the same?
Am
D
Will it make it eas - i - er on you, now,
Fmaj7
G
you got some - one to blame? You say
Chorus
C
Am
one love,
one life,

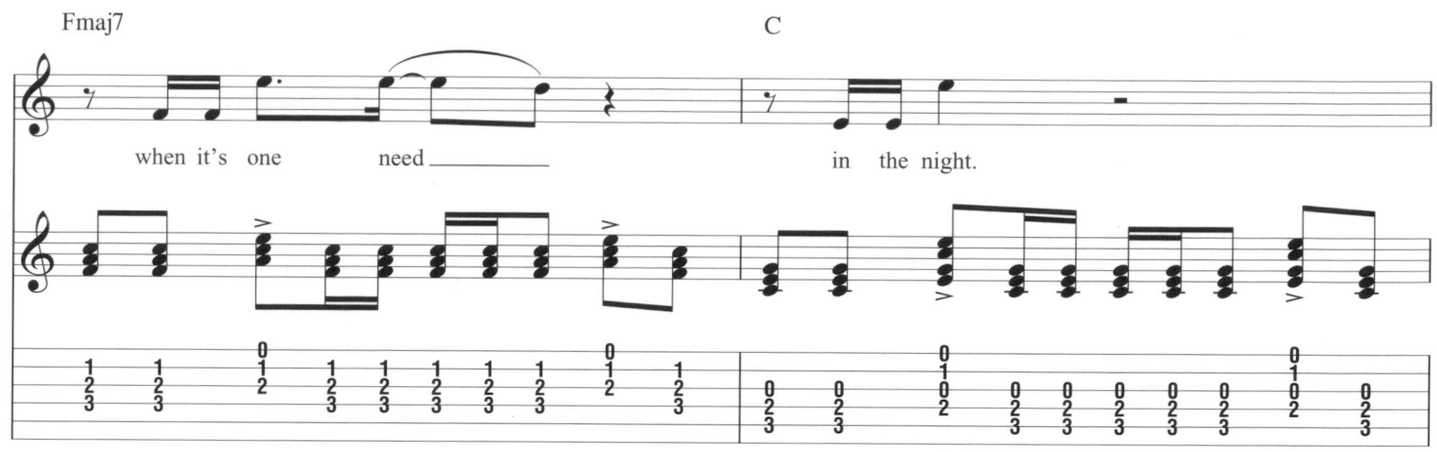
Fmaj7
C
when it's one need
in the night.

Am
One love,
we get to share it.

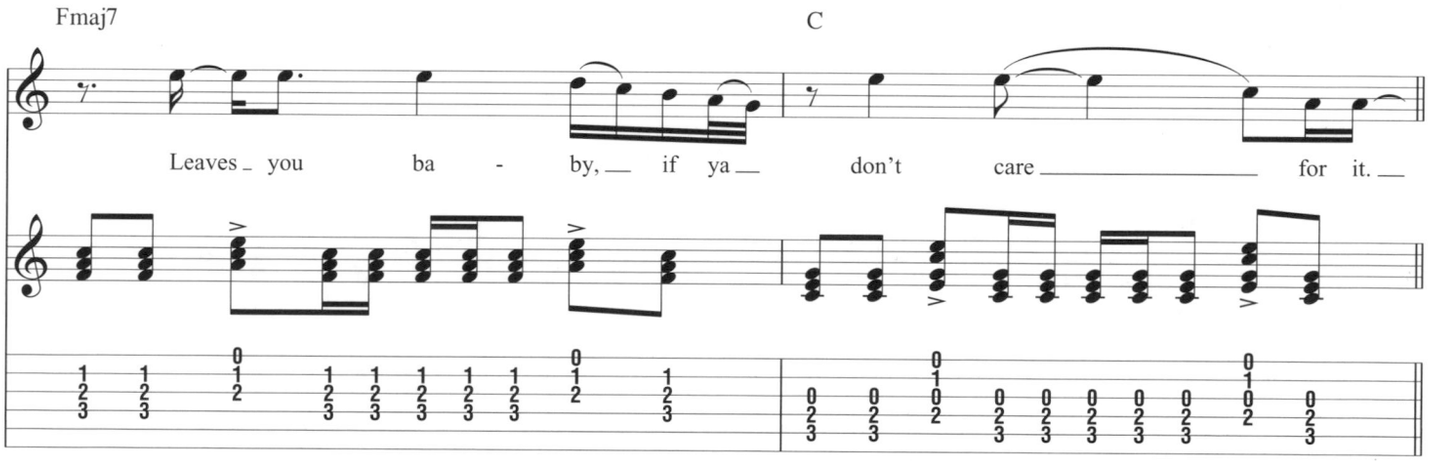
Fmaj7
C
Leaves you ba - by, if ya don't care for it.

Interlude

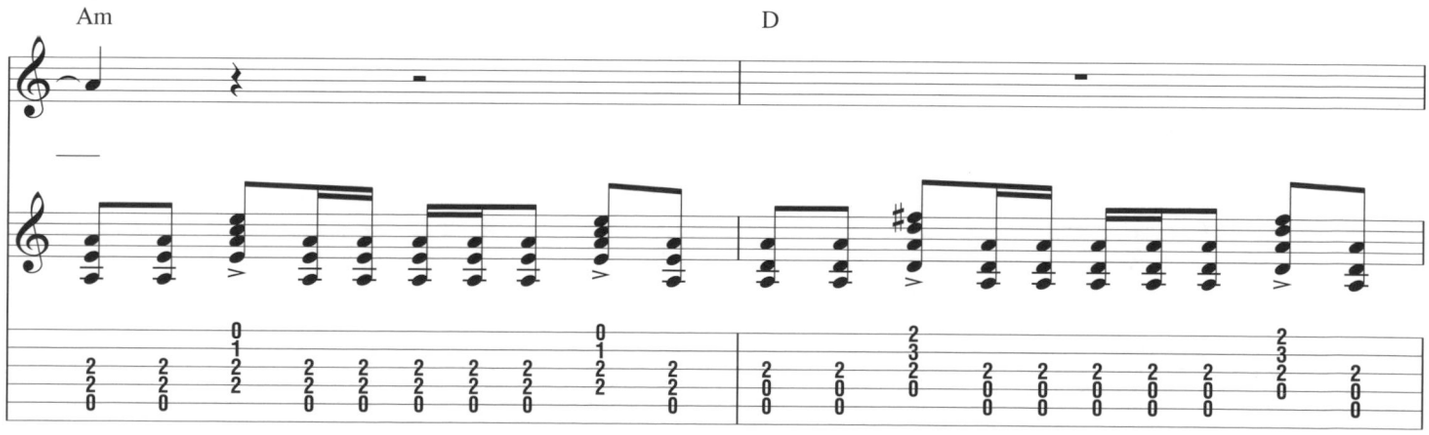
Am
D

Fmaj7
G
Verse
Am
D
2. Did I dis - ap - point you,
3. See additional lyrics
Fmaj7
G
or leave a bad taste in your mouth?
Am
D
You act like you nev - er had love,

Fmaj7
G
and you want me to go with - out.
Well, it's
See additional lyrics

Chorus

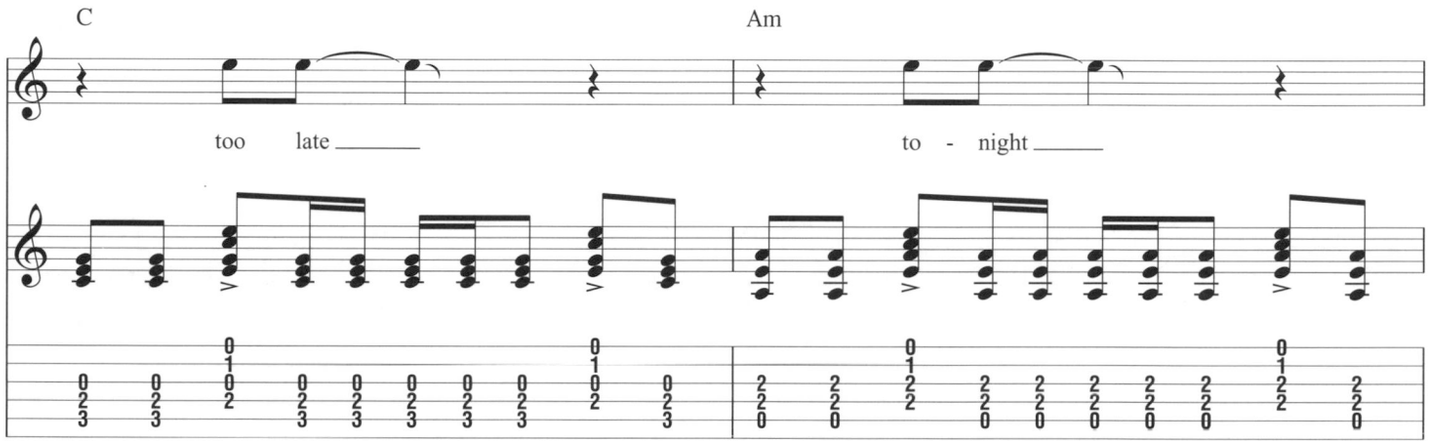
C
Am
too late
to - night

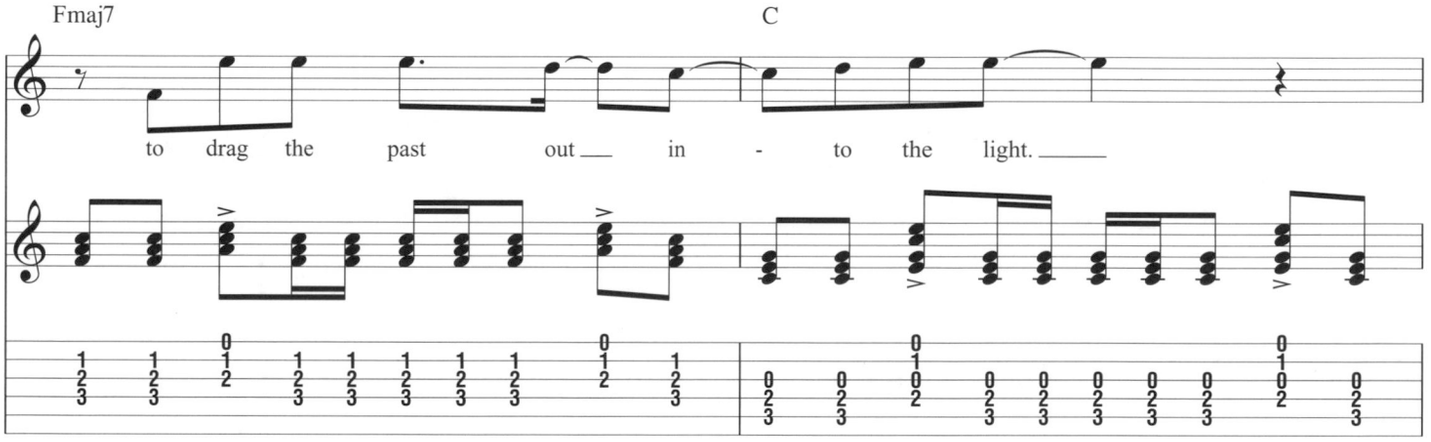
Fmaj7
C
to drag the past out in - to the light.

Am
We're one, but we're not the same. We get to

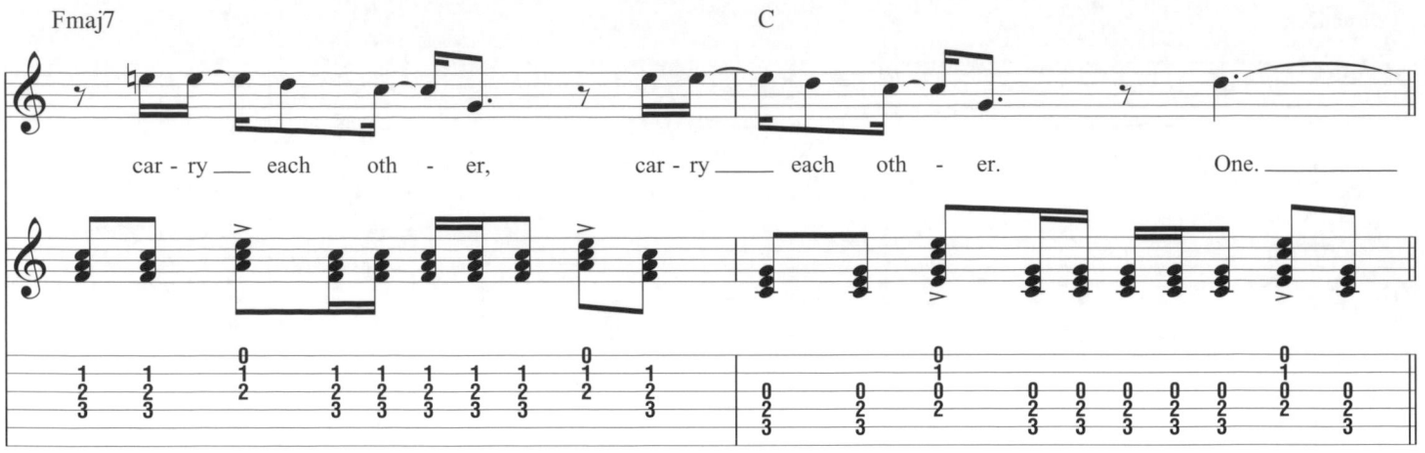

1.

Interlude

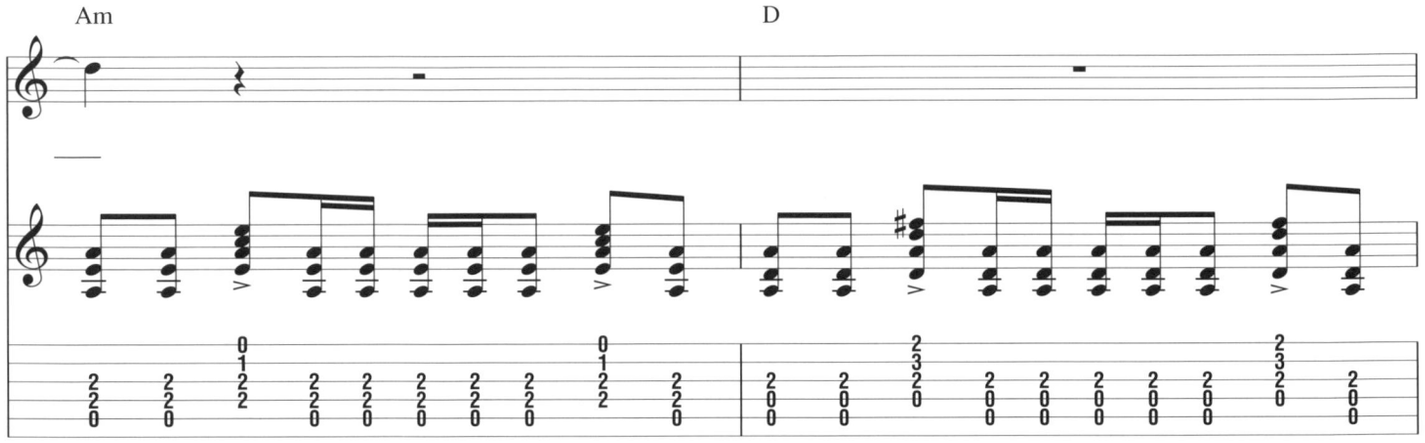

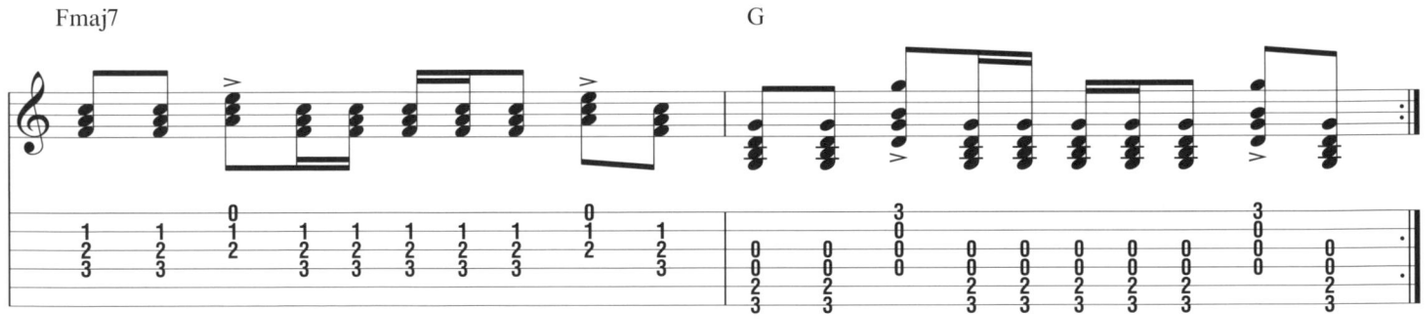

2.

Bridge

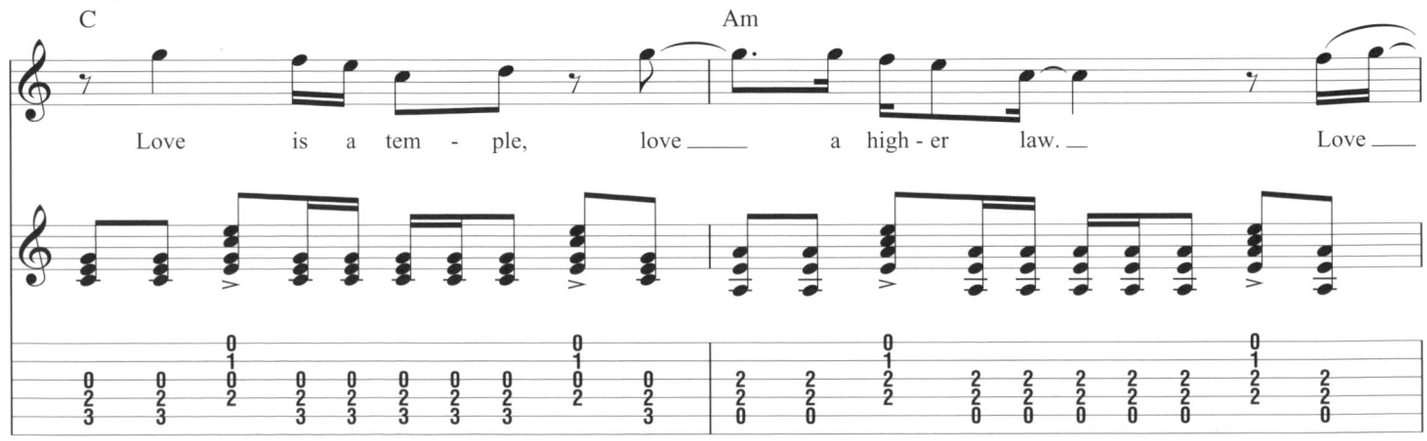

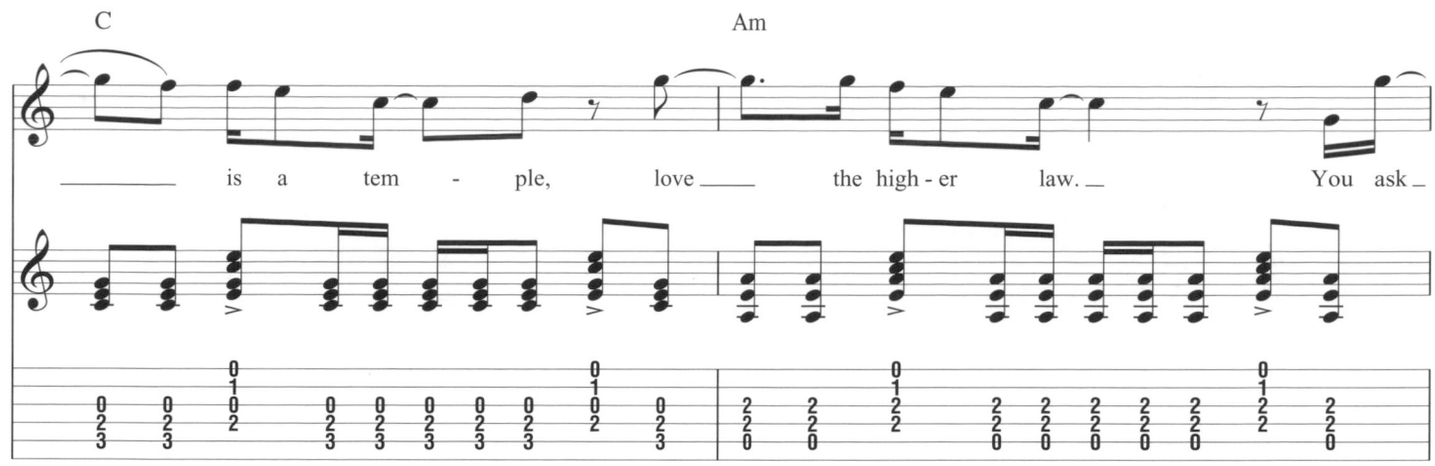
C
Am
is a tem - ple, love the high - er law. You ask

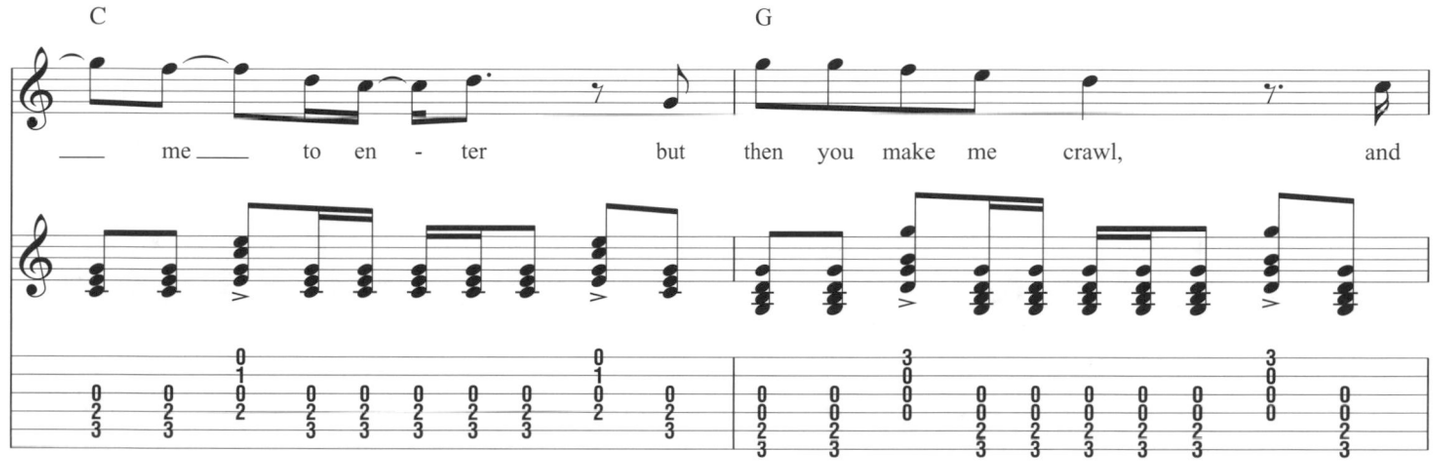
C
G
me to en - ter but then you make me crawl, and

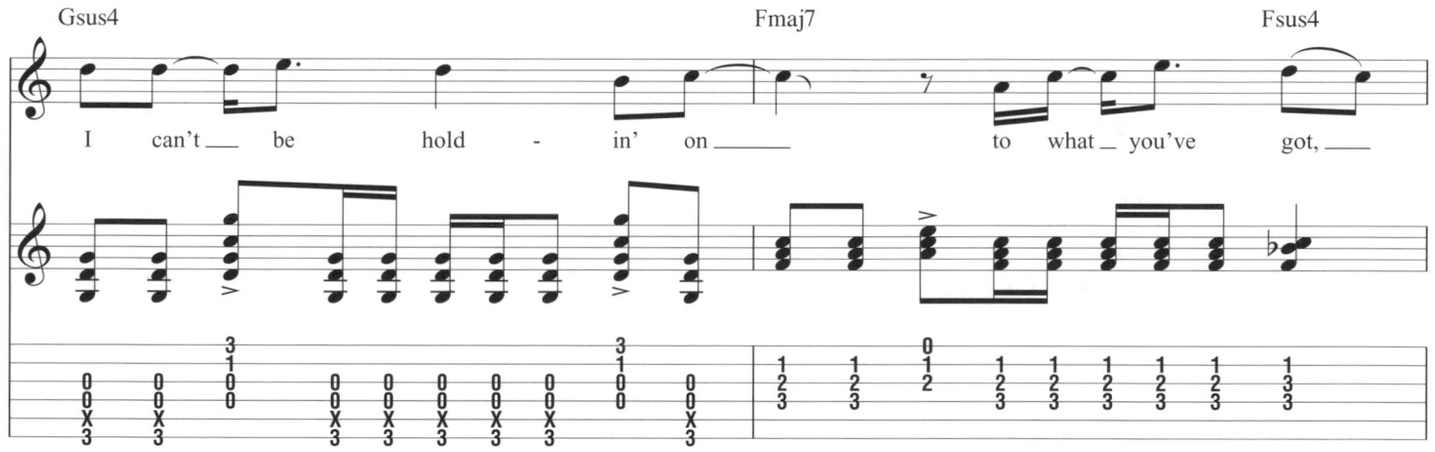
Gsus4
Fmaj7
Fsus4
I can't be hold - in' on to what you've got,

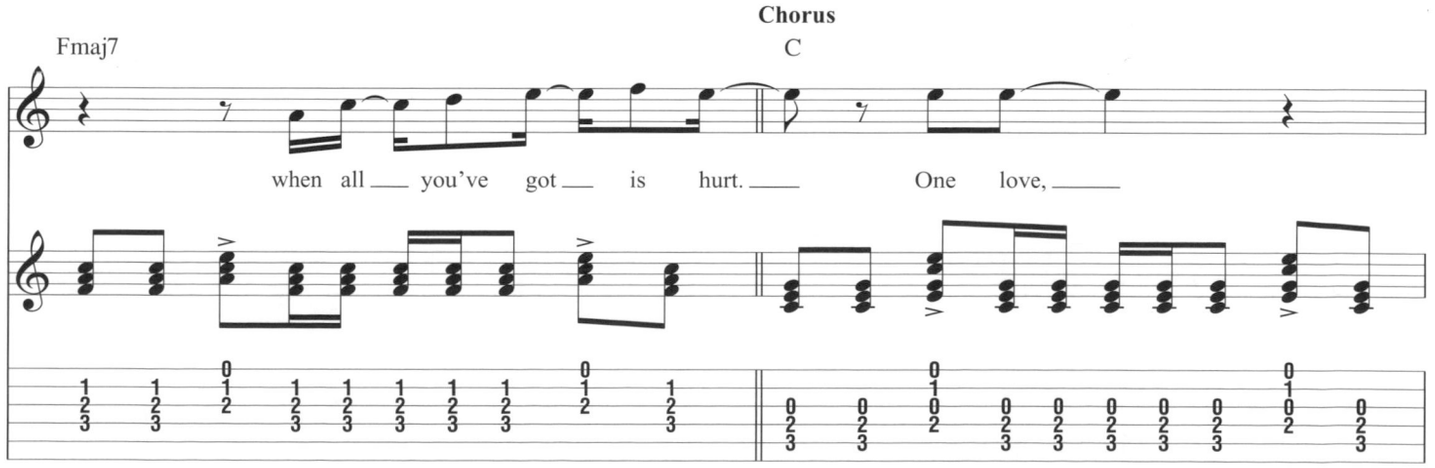
Chorus
Fmaj7
C
when all you've got is hurt. One love,

Am
Fmaj7
one blood,
one life,
you got to
C
do what you should.
One life,
Am
Fmaj7
with each oth - er.
Sis - ters,
C
bro - thers.
One life
but we're

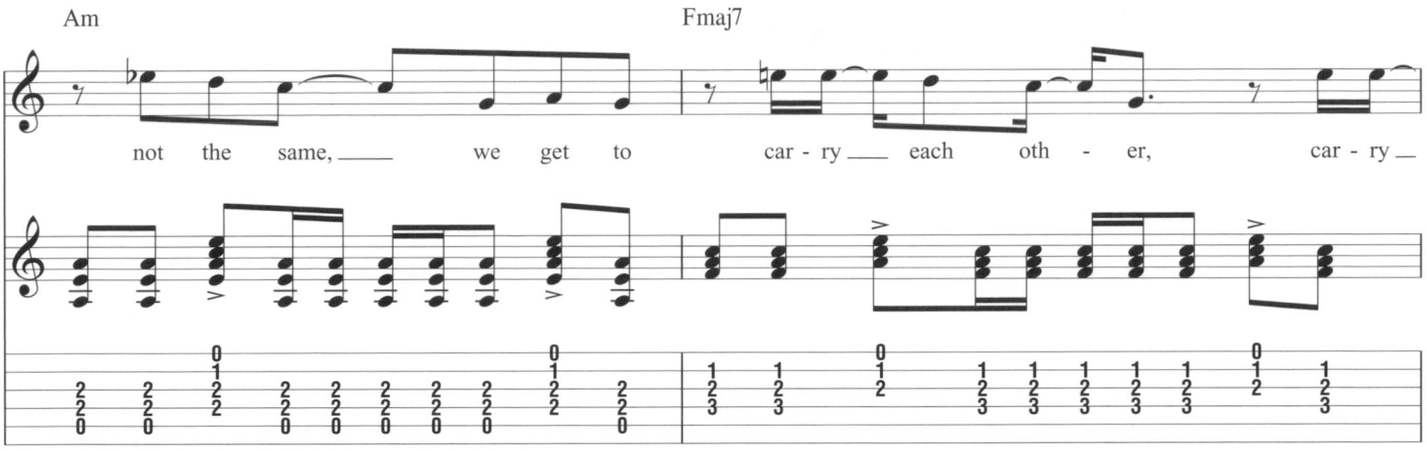

Outro

w/ Voc. ad lib. on repeats

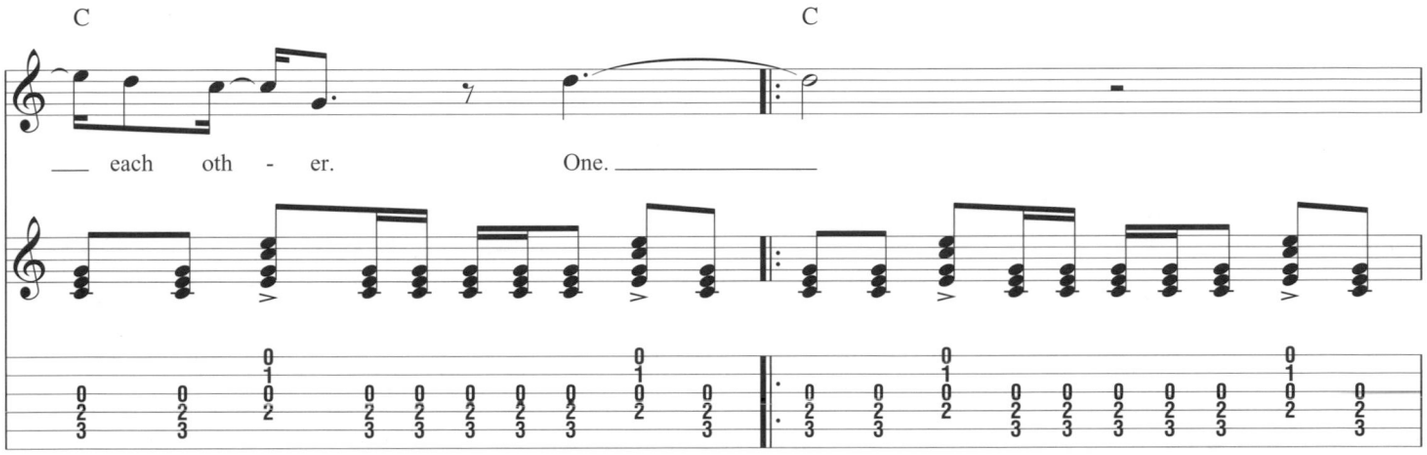

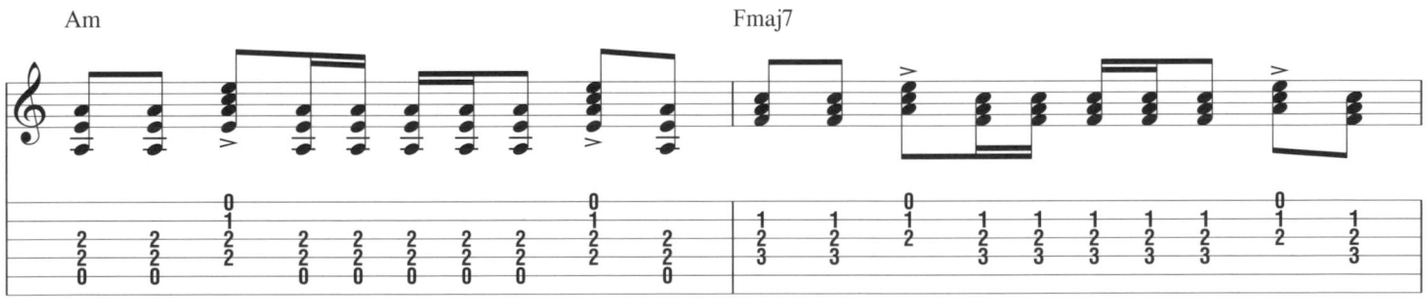

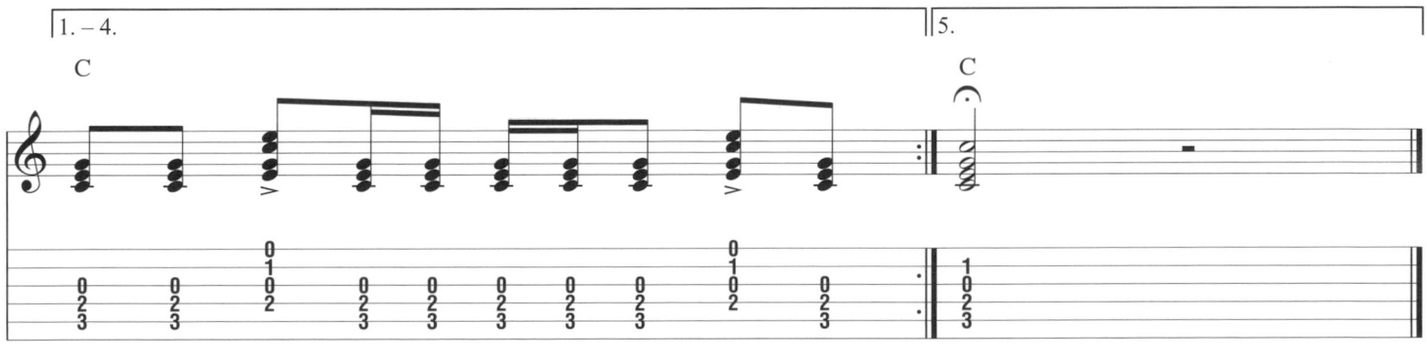

Additional Lyrics

3. Have you come here for forgiveness,
Have you come to raise the dead?
Have you come here to play Jesus,
To the lepers in your head?

Chorus Did I ask too much? More than a lot?
You gave me nothing, now it's all I got.
We're one, but we're not the same.
Well, we hurt each other, then we do it again.
You say...

The Scientist

Words and Music by Guy Berryman, Jon Buckland, Will Champion and Chris Martin

Capo I

Intro

Slowly ♩ = 74

*Dm7 (C♯m7) | B♭ (A) | F (E)

mf

*Symbols in parentheses represent chord names respective to capoed guitar.
Symbols above reflect actual sounding chords. Capoed fret is "0" in tab.

Verse

Fsus2 (Esus2) | Dm7 (C♯m7) | B♭ (A)

1. Come up to meet you, tell you I'm sor -

F (E) | Fsus2 (Esus2) | Dm7 (C♯m7)

- ry, you don't know how love - ly you are. I had to find

Copyright © 2002 by Universal Music Publishing MGB Ltd.
All Rights in the United States Administered by Universal Music - MGB Songs
International Copyright Secured All Rights Reserved

B♭ (A)
F (E)
Fsus2 (Esus2)
you, tell you I need you, tell you I'll set you a - part.
Dm7 (C♯m7)
B♭ (A)
F (E)
Tell me your se - crets and ask me your ques - tions, oh, let's go back
Fsus2 (Esus2)
Dm7 (C♯m7)
B♭ (A)
to the start. Run - nin' in cir - cles, com - ing up tails,
Chorus
F (E)
Fsus2 (Esus2)
B♭ (A)
heads on a sci - ence a - part. No - bod - y said

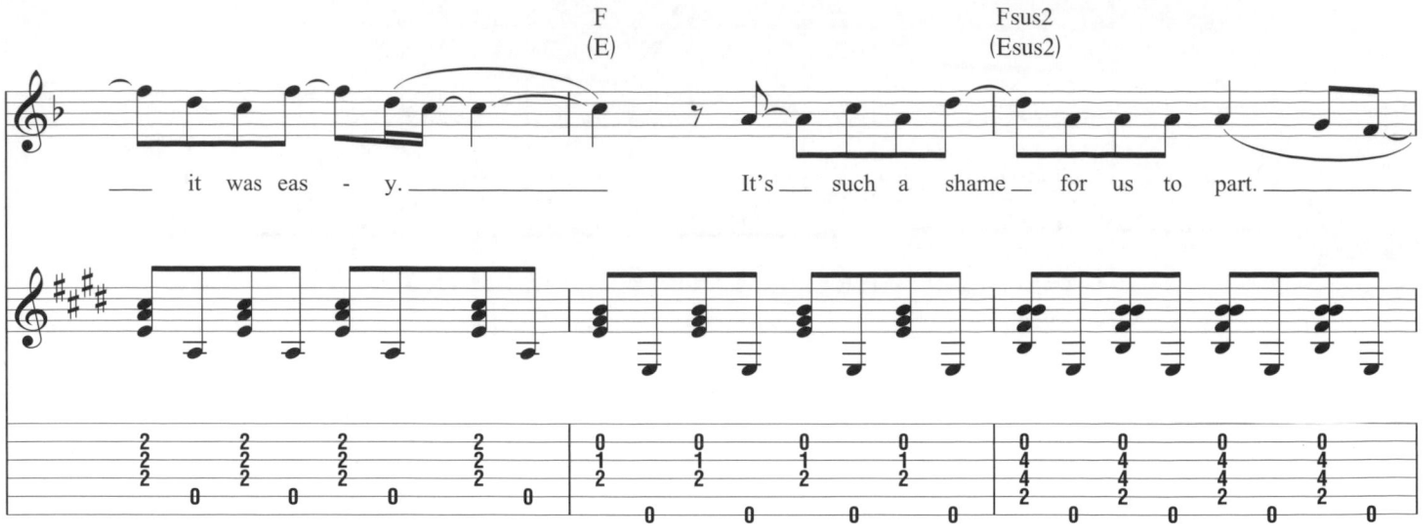
F
(E)
Fsus2
(Esus2)
it was eas - y.
It's such a shame for us to part.

B♭
(A)
F
(E)
No - bod - y said it was eas - y.
No one ev - er

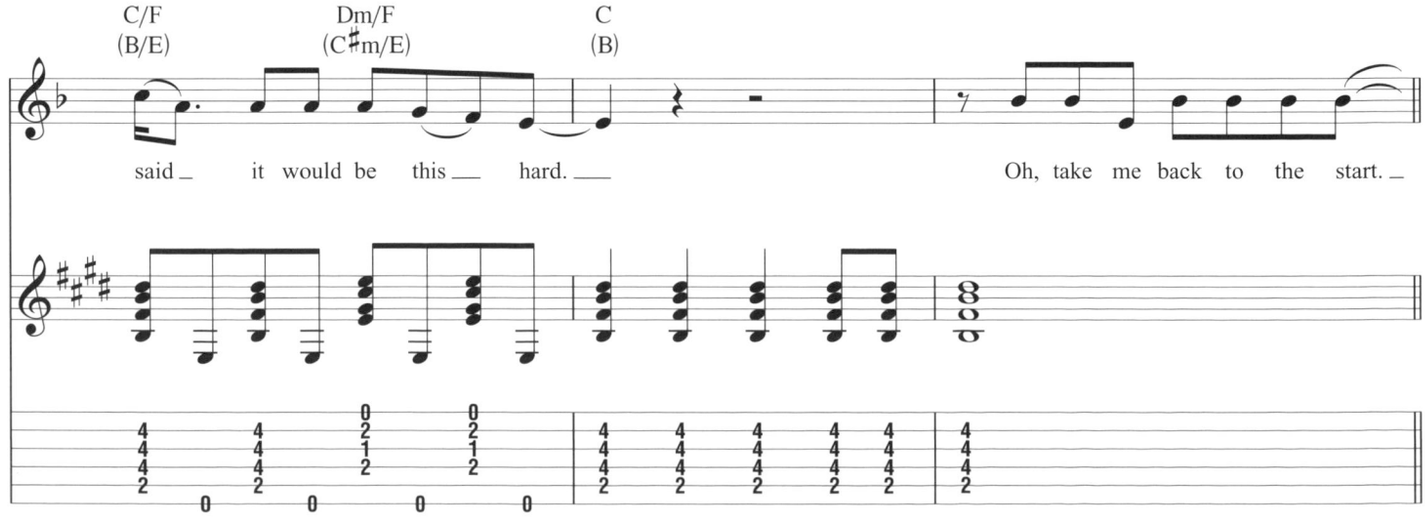
C/F
(B/E)
Dm/F
(C♯m/E)
C
(B)
said it would be this hard.
Oh, take me back to the start.

Interlude
F
(E)
B♭
(A)
F
(E)
Dm7
(C♯m7)
B♭
(A)
F
(E)
Fsus2
(Esus2)
Verse
Dm7
(C♯m7)
2. I was just guess -
B♭
(A)
F
(E)
Fsus2
(Esus2)
- in' at num-bers and fig - ures, pull-ing your puz - zles a - part.

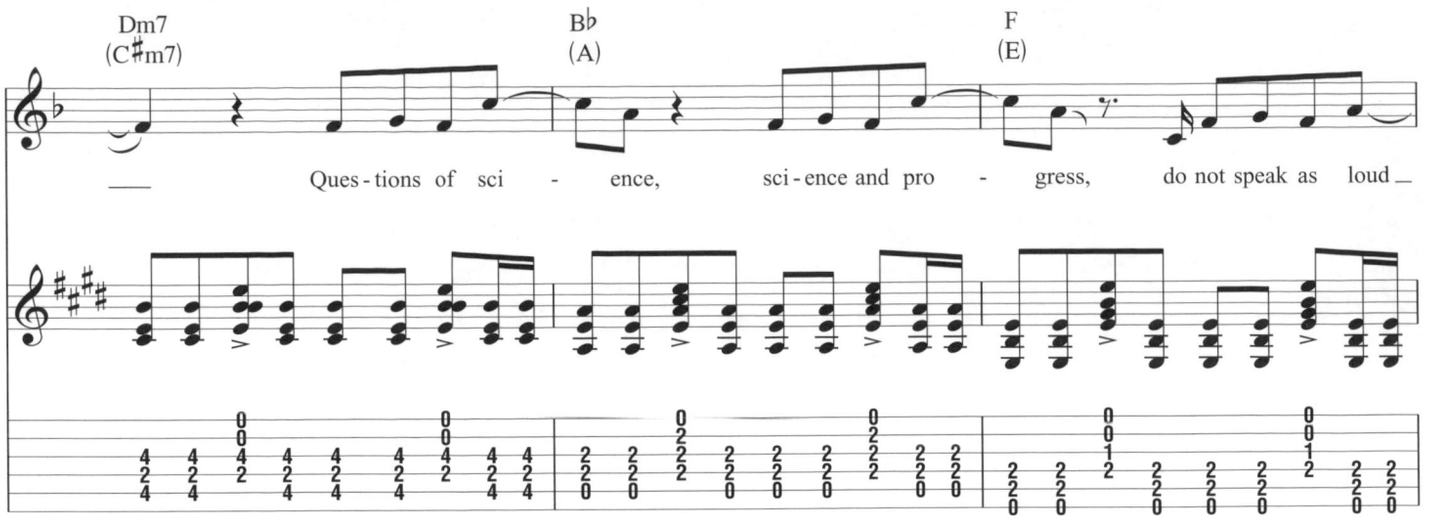
Dm7
(C♯m7)
B♭
(A)
F
(E)
Ques-tions of sci - ence, sci-ence and pro - gress, do not speak as loud

Fsus2
(Esus2)
Dm7
(C♯m7)
B♭
(A)
as my heart. Tell me you love me, come back and haunt

F
(E)
Fsus2
(Esus2)
Dm7
(C♯m7)
me, oh, when I rush to the start. Run-nin' in cir -

B♭ (A)
F (E)
Fsus2 (Esus2)
- cles, chas-ing our tails, com - in' back as we are.
Chorus
B♭ (A)
F (E)
No - bod - y said it was eas - y. Oh, it's such a shame
Fsus2 (Esus2)
B♭ (A)
for us to part. No - bod - y said it was eas - y.
F (E)
C/F (B/E)
Dm/F (C♯m/E)
C (B)
No one ev - er said it would be so hard.

Interlude
F
(E)
B♭
(A)
I'm go - in' back to the start.
F
(E)
Dm7
(C♯m7)
B♭
(A)
F
(E)
Outro
Dm7
(C♯m7)
B♭
(A)
F
(E)
Oh, ooh.

Dm7
(C♯m7)
B♭
(A)
Ah, ooh.
F
(E)
Dm7
(C♯m7)
Oh, ooh.
B♭
(A)
F
(E)
Dm7
(C♯m7)
B♭
(A)
F
(E)
Oh, ooh.
mp

Sunny Came Home

Words and Music by Shawn Colvin and John Leventhal

© 1996 WB MUSIC CORP., SCRED SONGS LTD. and LEV-A-TUNES
All Rights for SCRED SONGS LTD. Administered by WB MUSIC CORP.
All Rights for LEV-A-TUNES Administered by DOWNTOWN DLJ SONGS
All Rights Reserved Used by Permission

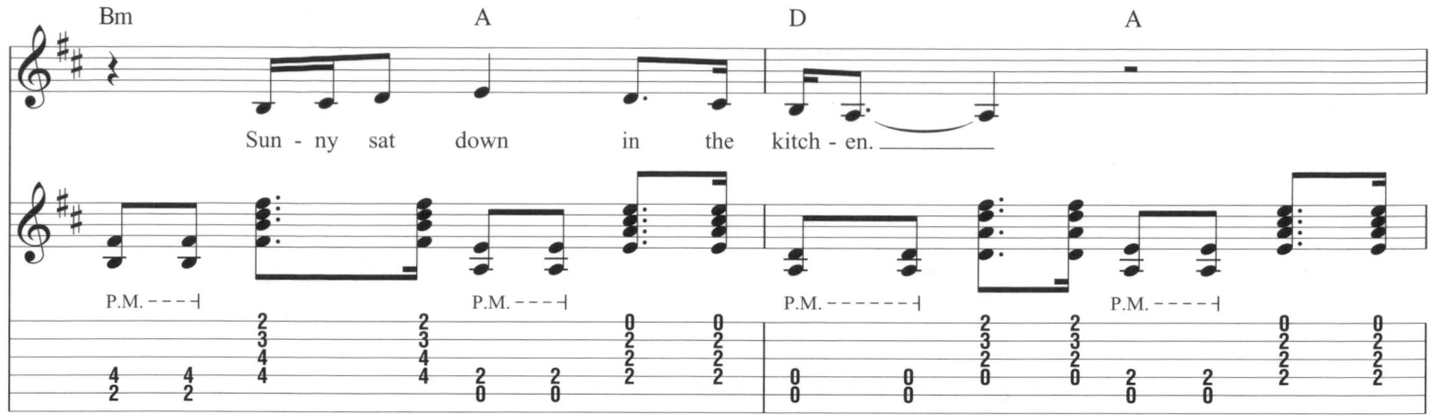
Bm A D A
Sun - ny sat down in the kitch - en.
P.M.
P.M.
P.M.
P.M.

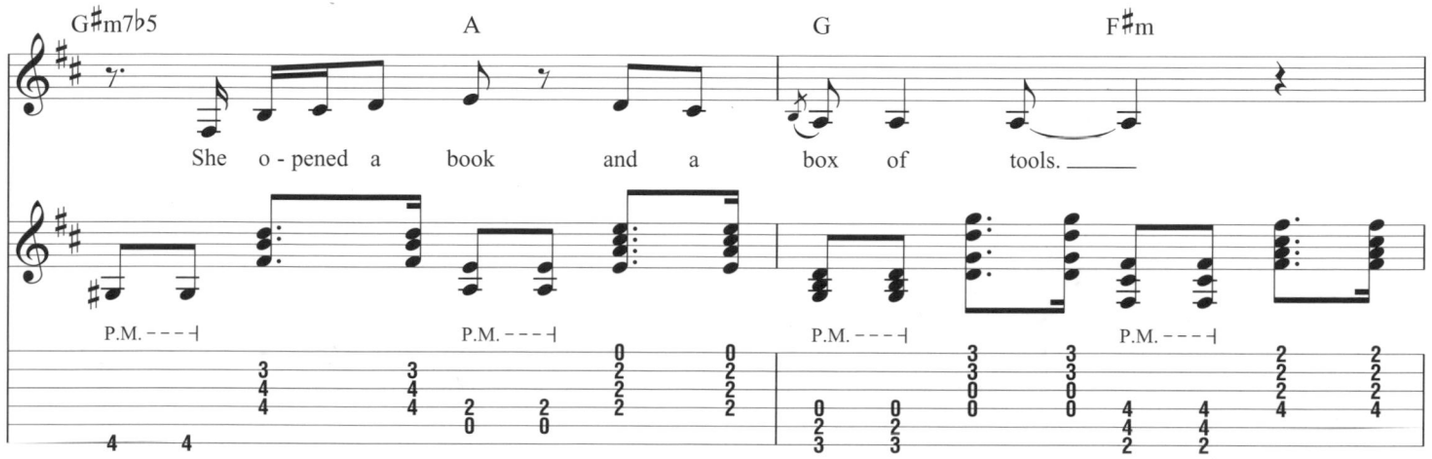
G♯m7♭5 A G F♯m
She o - pened a book and a box of tools.
P.M.
P.M.
P.M.
P.M.

Em Bm G sus2 add♯4 G
Sun - ny came home with a mis - sion. She says, "Days

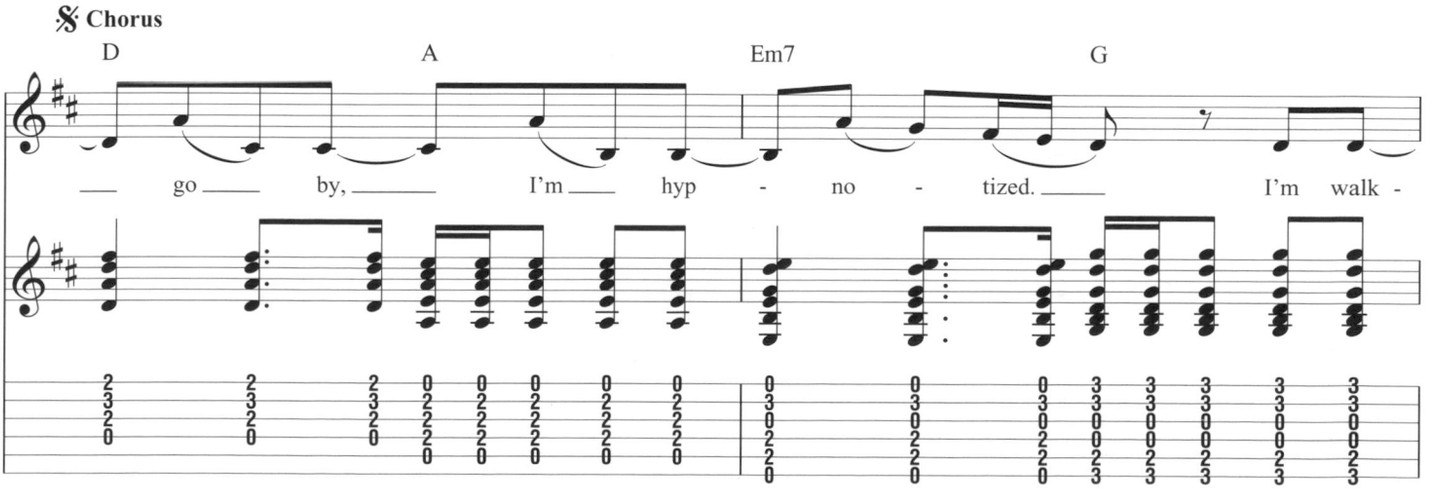
𝄋 Chorus
D A Em7 G
go by, I'm hyp - no - tized. I'm walk -

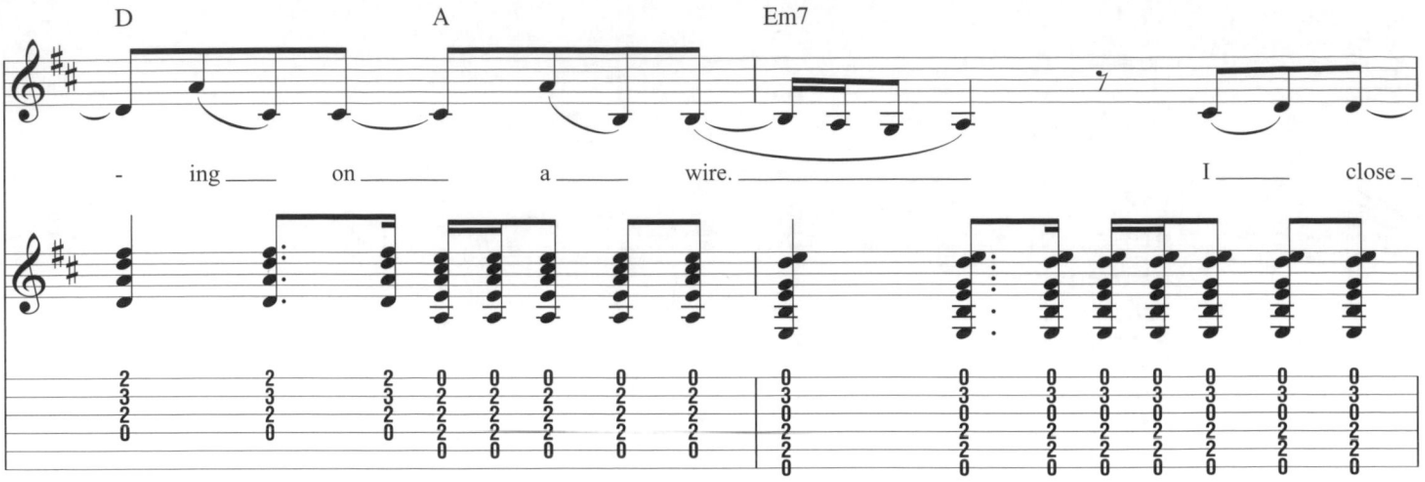

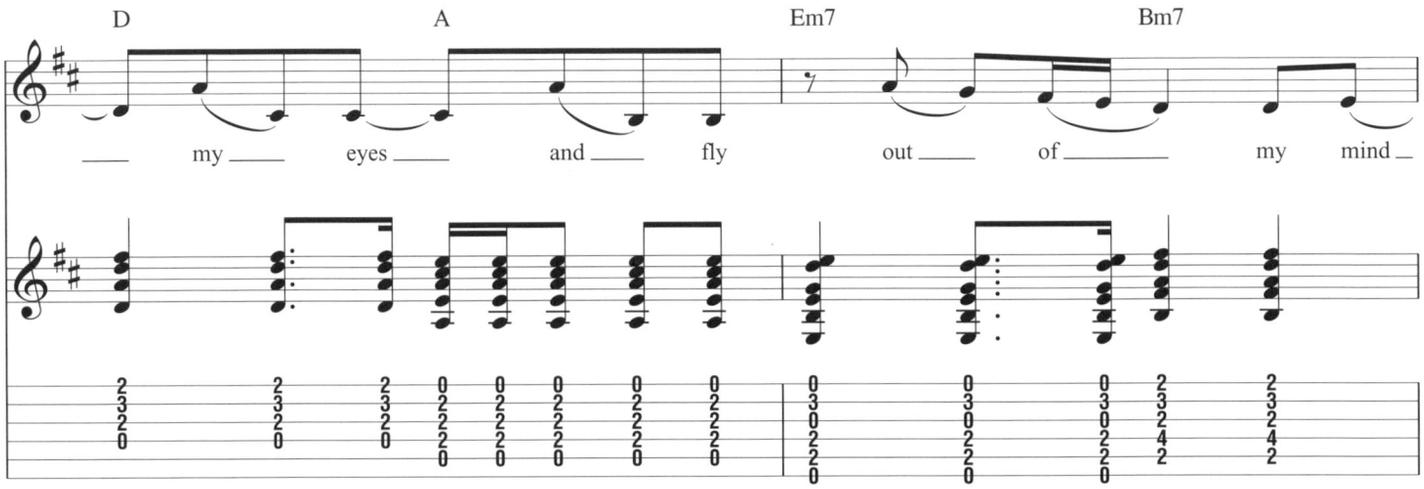

To Coda

Interlude

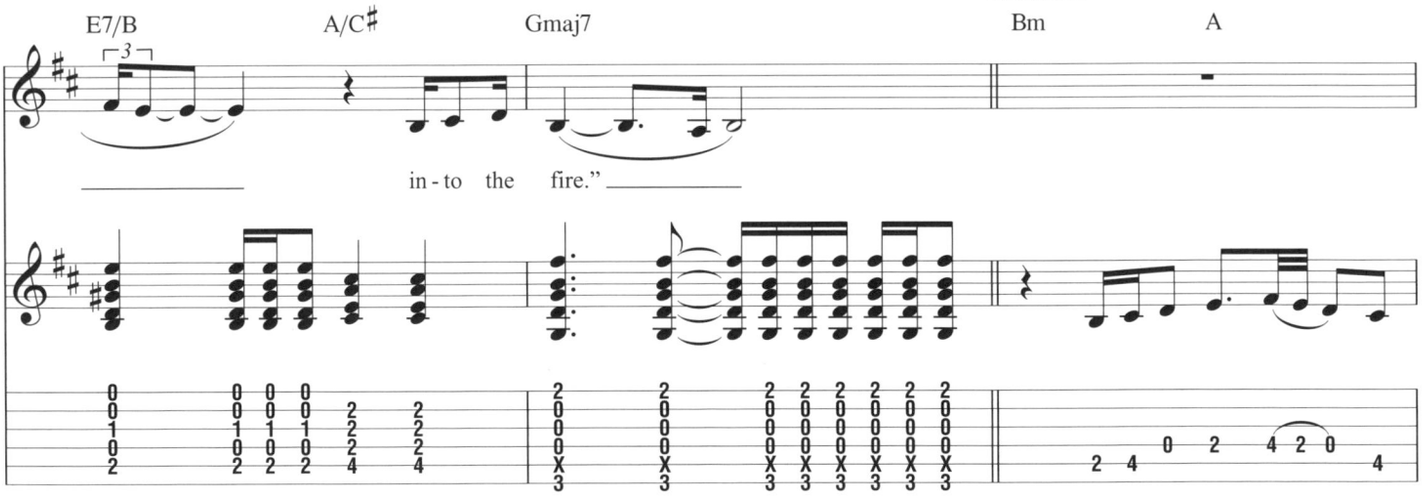

Verse
Bm A D A
2. Sun - ny came home with a list of names.
P.M.
Bm A D F♯m
She did - n't be - lieve in tran - scen - dence.
P.M.
G A Bm A/C♯
"And it's time for a few small re - pairs," she said.
P.M.
D.S. al Coda
Em Bm G sus2 add♯4 G
Sun - ny came home with a ven - geance. She says, "Days

Coda
Bridge
Gmaj7
A/C♯
F♯m
fire."
Get the kids and bring
G6/9
A/C♯
F♯m
a sweat - er. Dry is good and wind
G6/9
A/C♯
F♯m
is bet - ter. Count the years; you al -

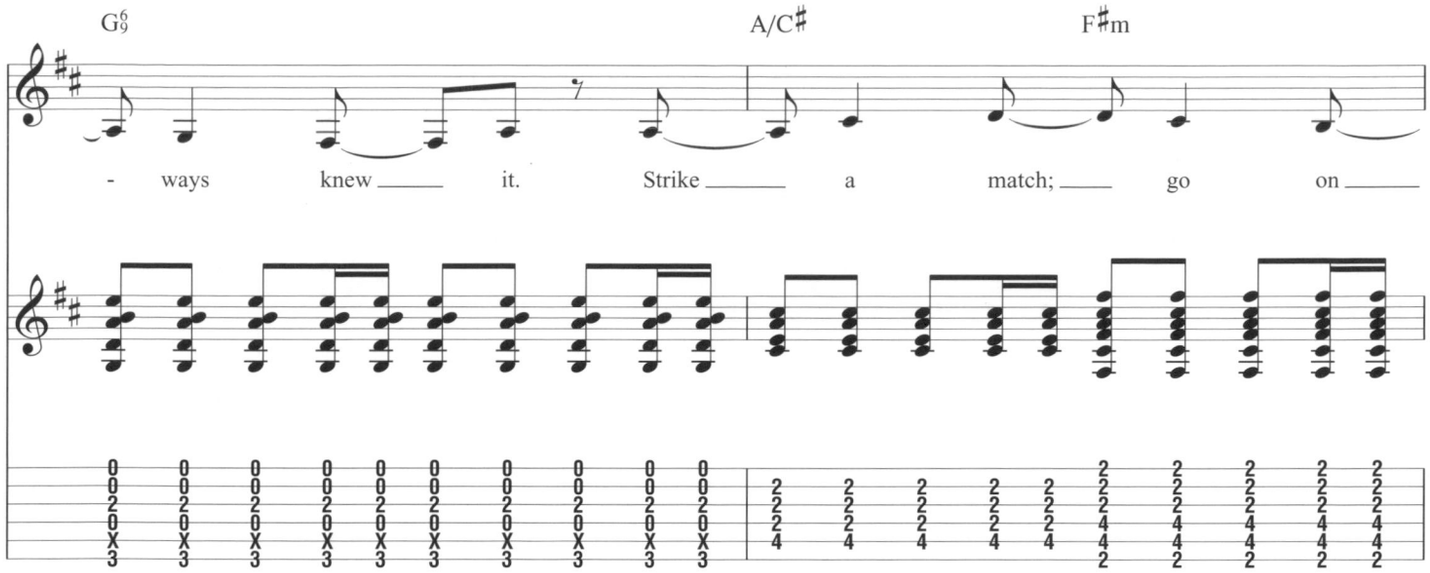
G6/9
A/C♯
F♯m
- ways knew it. Strike a match; go on

Chorus

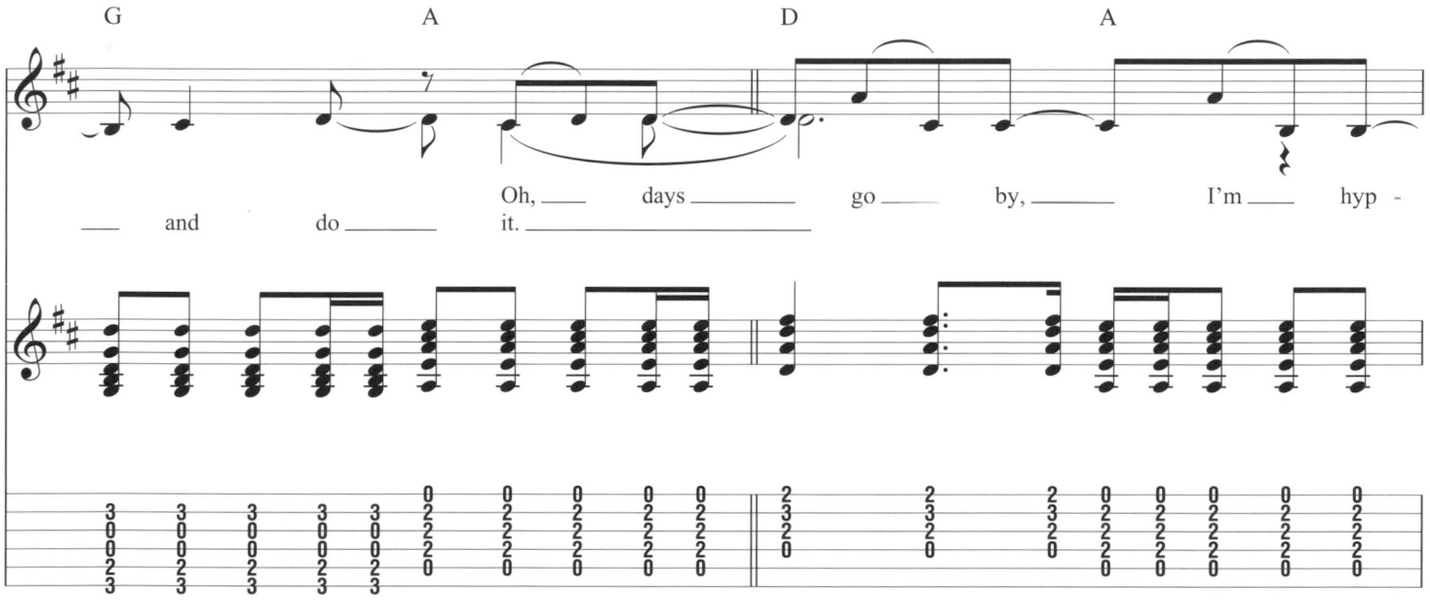
G
A
D
A
Oh, days go by, I'm hyp -
and do it.

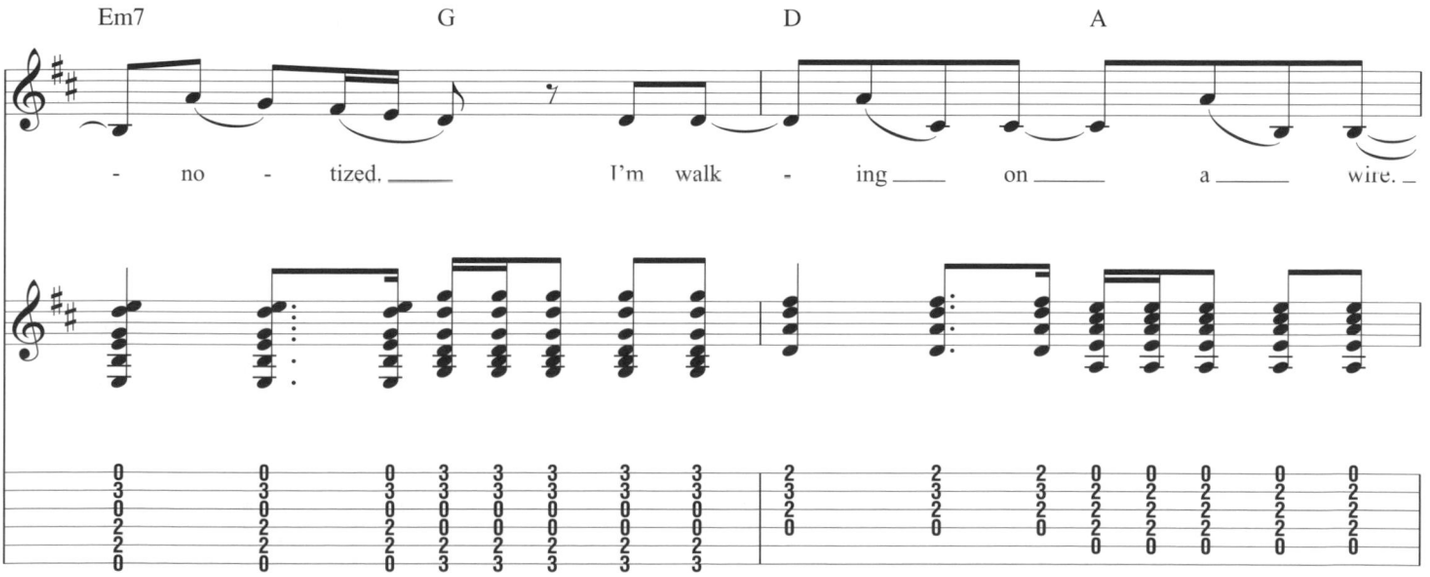
Em7
G
D
A
- no - tized. I'm walk - ing on a wire.

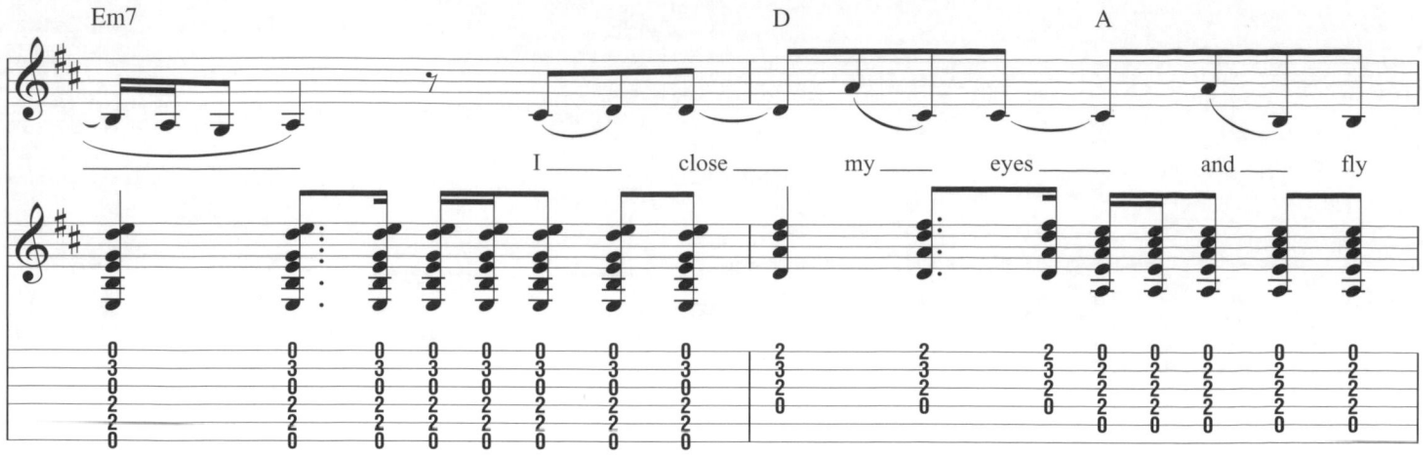
Em7
D
A
I close my eyes and fly

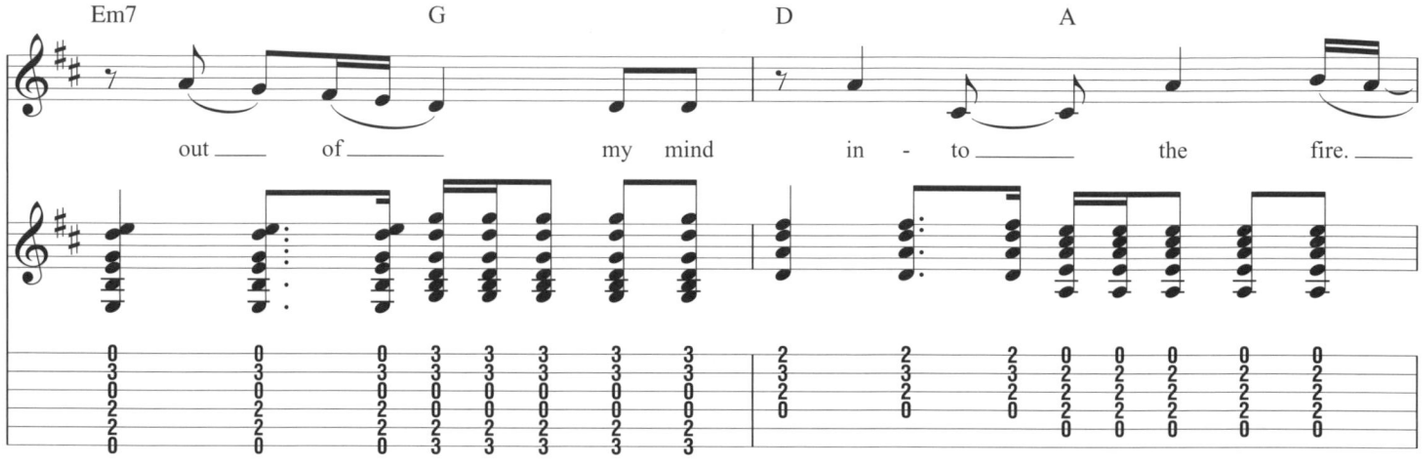
Em7
G
D
A
out of my mind in - to the fire.

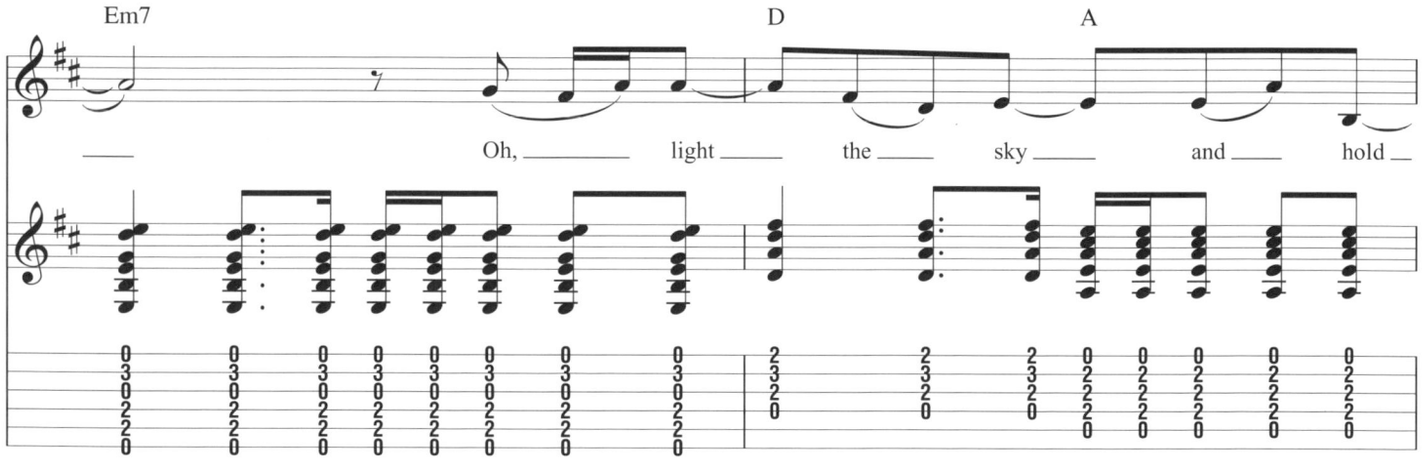
Em7
D
A
Oh, light the sky and hold

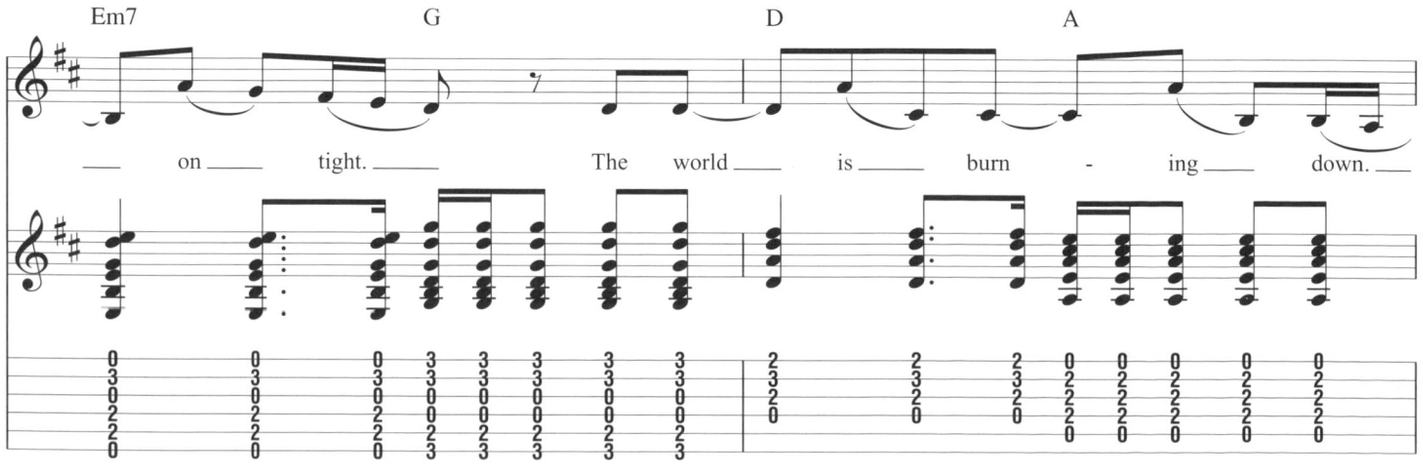
Em7
G
D
A
on tight. The world is burn - ing down.

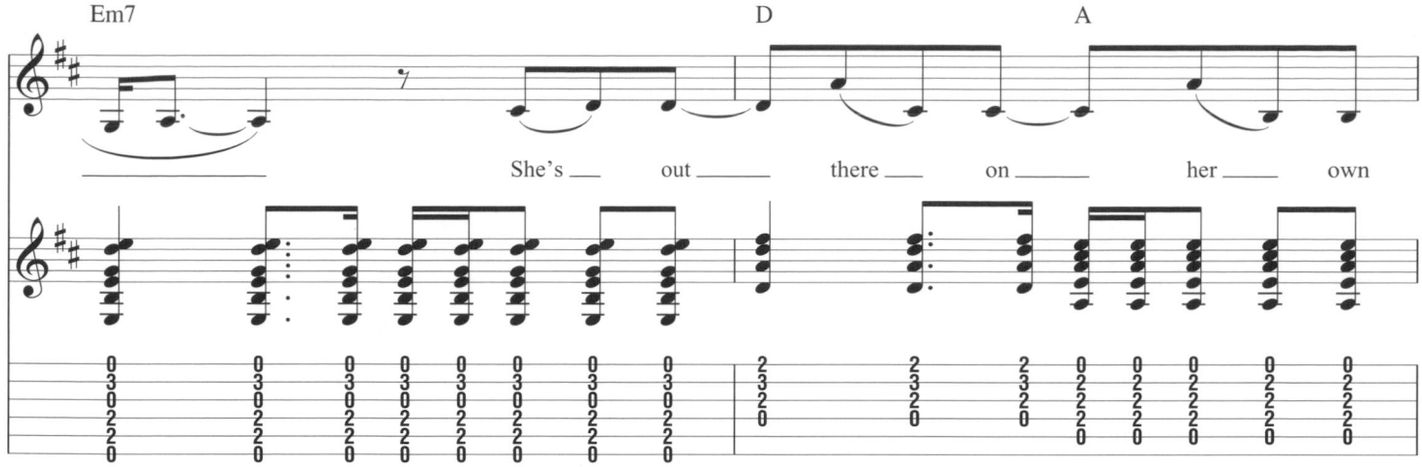
Em7
D
A
She's out there on her own

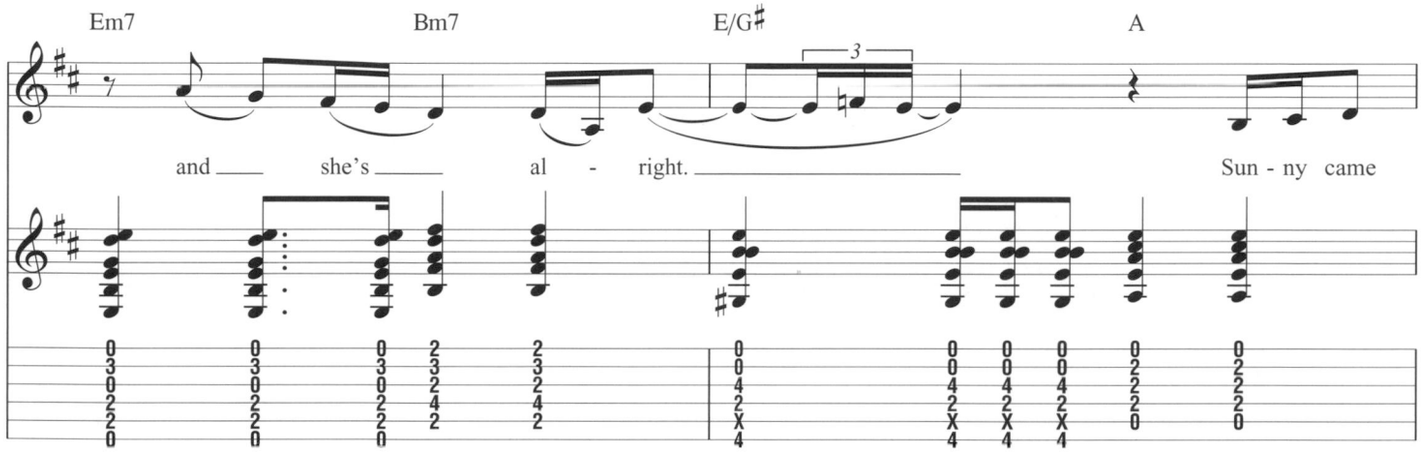
Em7
Bm7
E/G♯
A
and she's al - right.
Sun - ny came

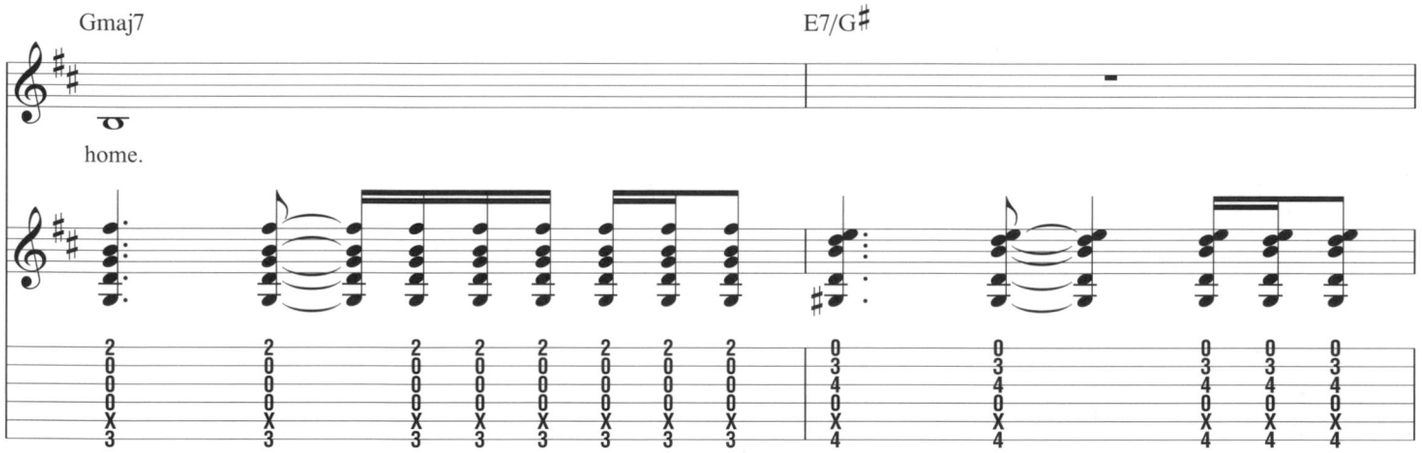
Gmaj7
E7/G♯
home.

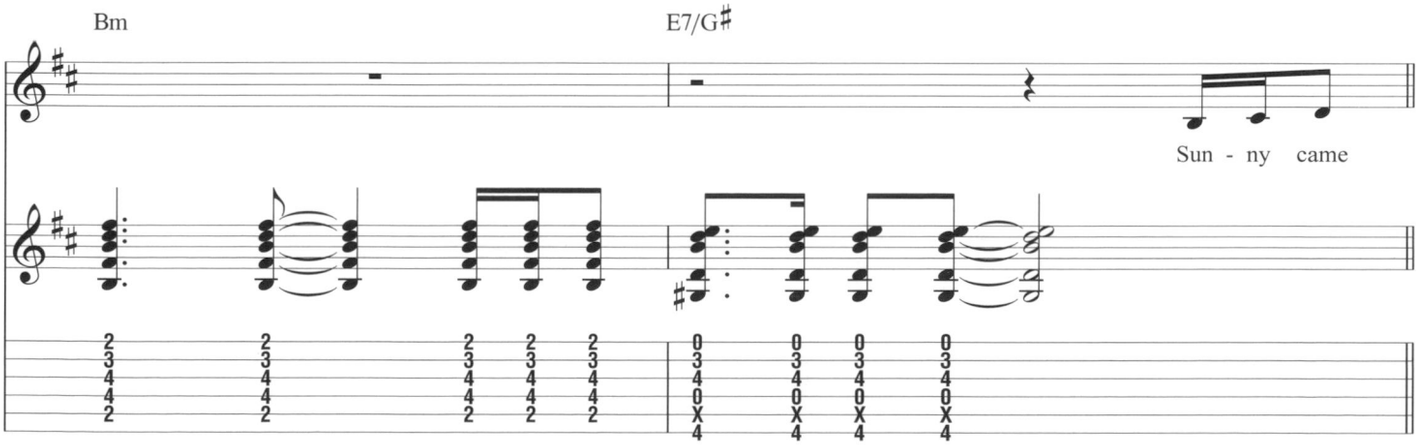
Bm
E7/G♯
Sun - ny came

Outro

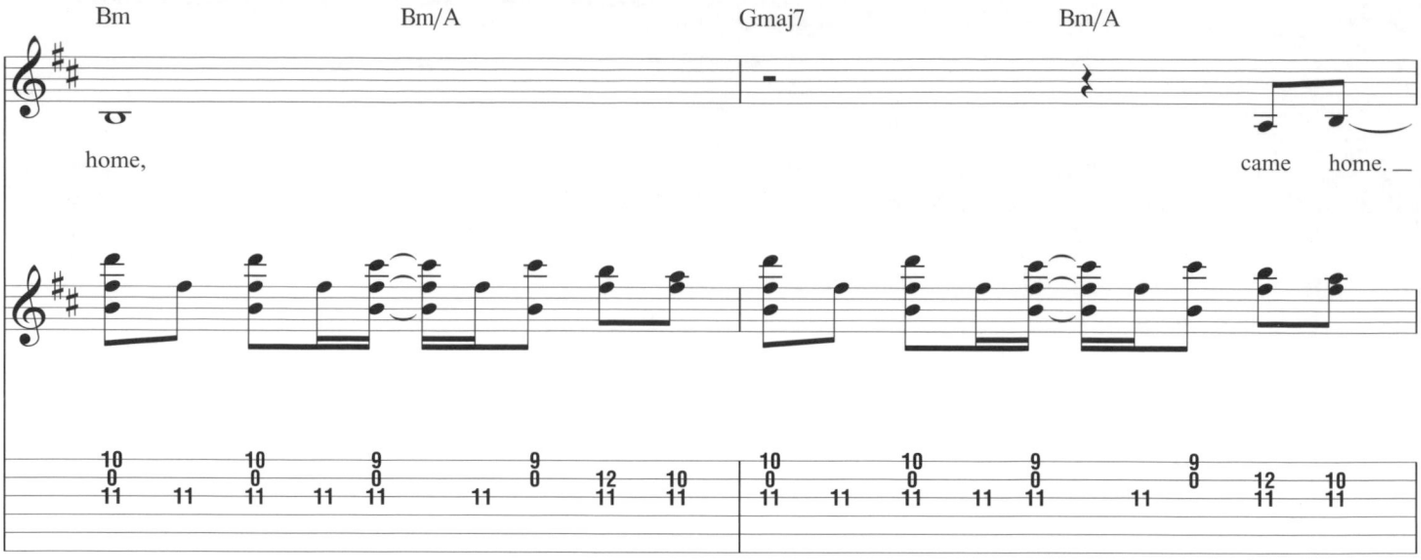
Bm
Bm/A
Gmaj7
Bm/A
home,
came home.

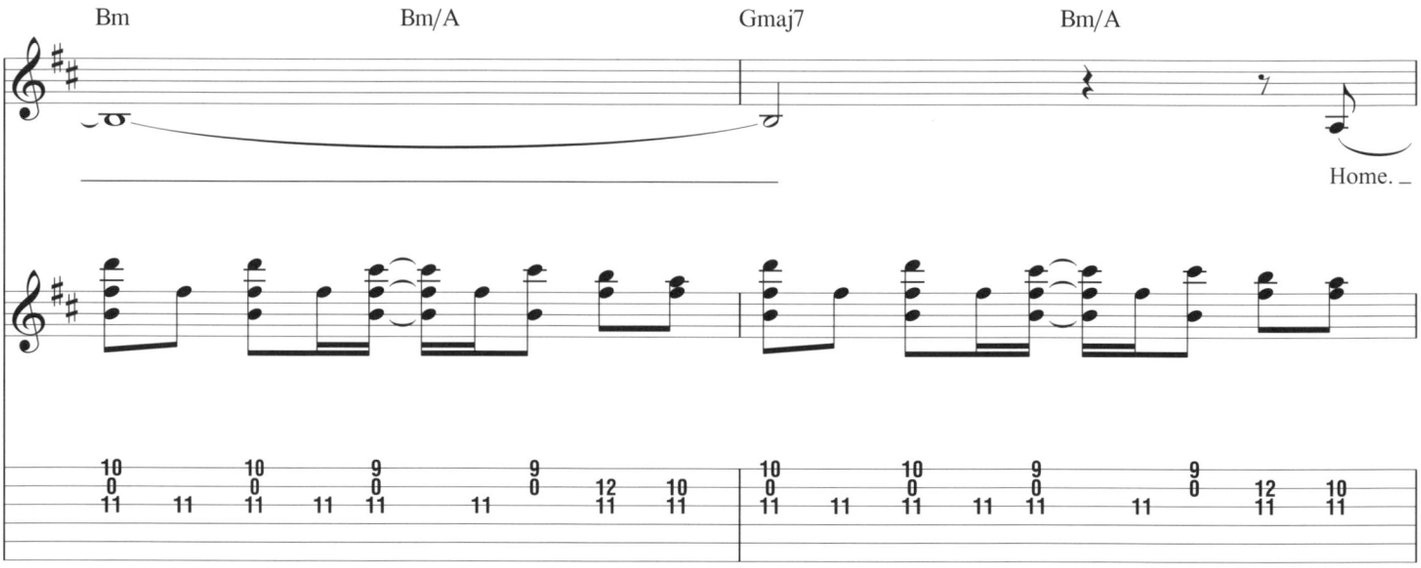
Bm
Bm/A
Gmaj7
Bm/A
Home.

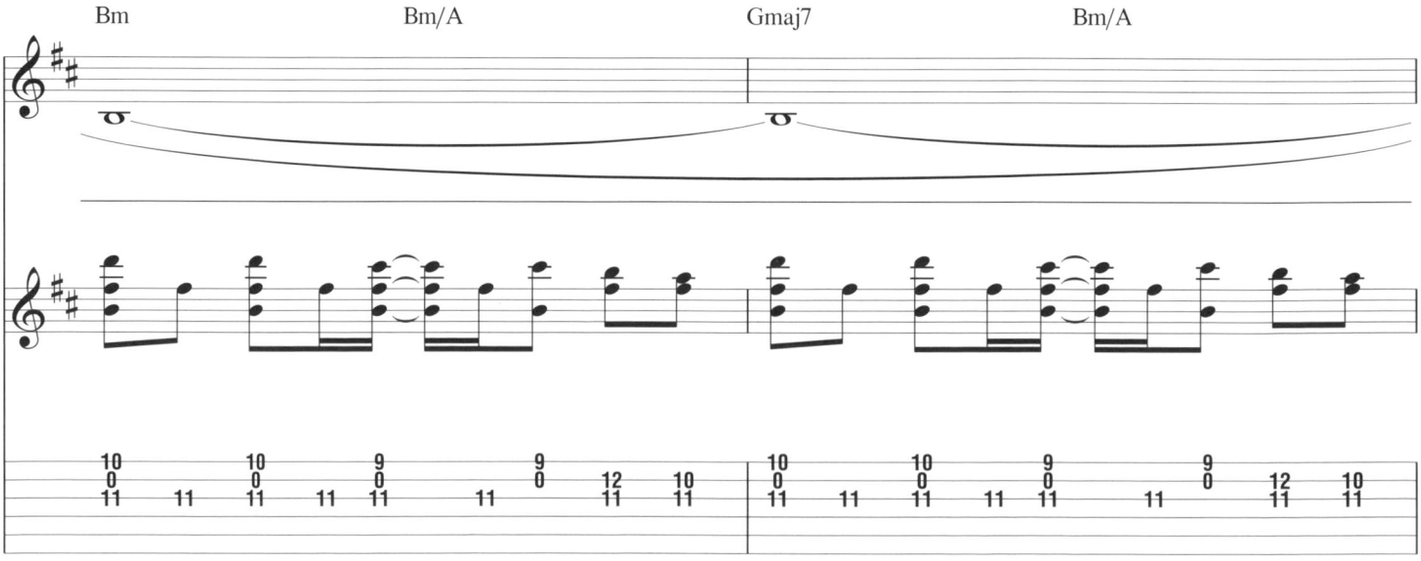
Bm
Bm/A
Gmaj7
Bm/A

Bm/E
Gmaj7
Bm
Bm/F♯
Bm/A
Bm/E
Gmaj7
Bsus2

What's Up

Words and Music by Linda Perry

Copyright © 1992 Sony/ATV Music Publishing LLC and Stuck In The Throat Music
All Rights Administered by Sony/ATV Music Publishing LLC, 424 Church Street, Suite 1200, Nashville, TN 37219
International Copyright Secured All Rights Reserved

Verse
A
Bm
1. Twen-ty five years and my life is still try'n' to get up that great big hill of hope
dist. off

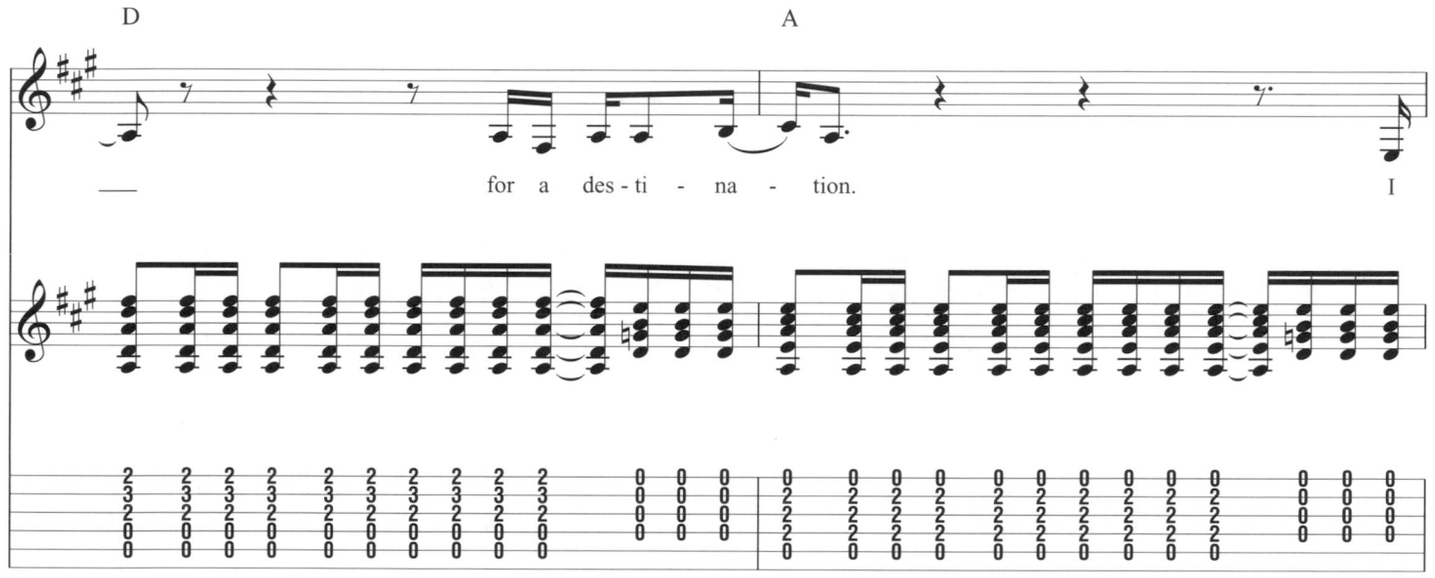
D
A
for a des-ti-na-tion. I

Bm
real-ized quick-ly when I knew I should, that the world was made up of this broth-er-hood of man,

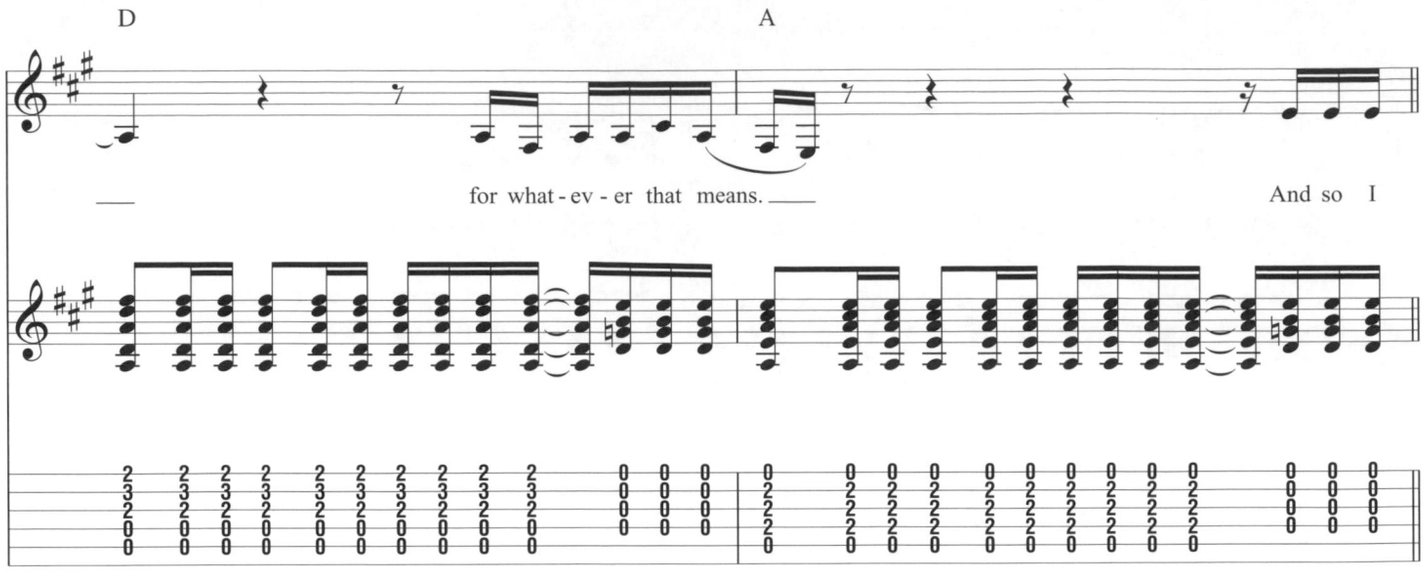
D
A
for what - ev - er that means.
And so I

𝄋 **Pre-Chorus**

A
Bm
cry some - times when I'm ly - ing in bed just to get it all out, what's in my head, and I,

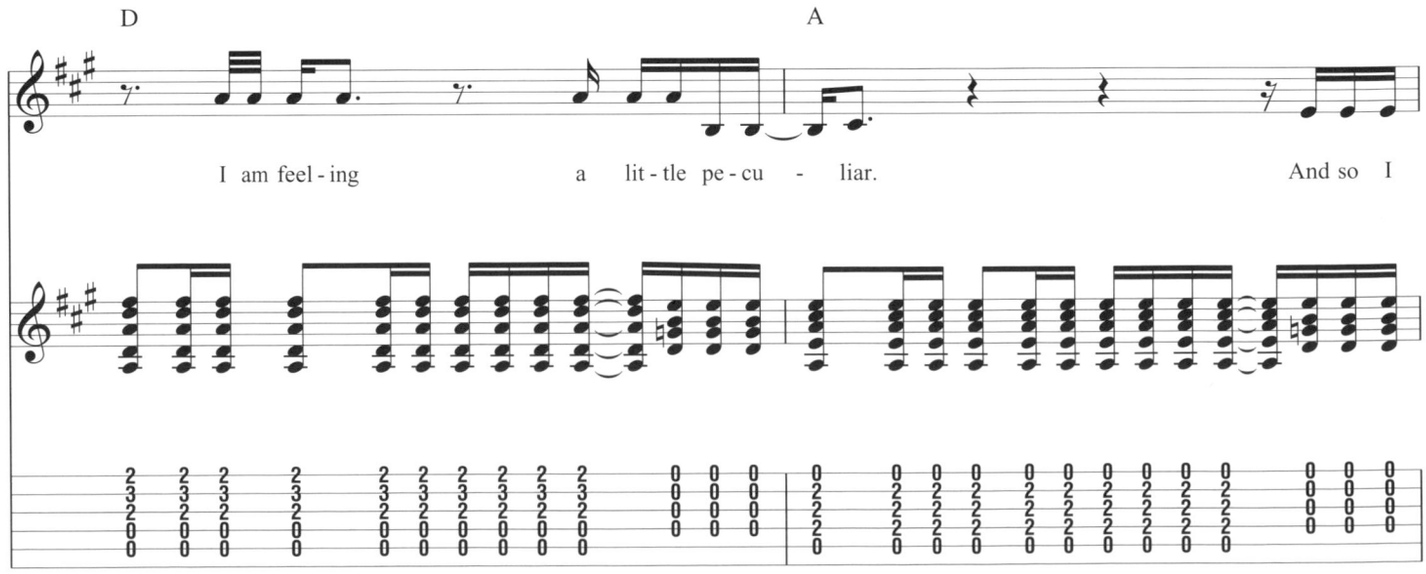
D
A
I am feel - ing a lit - tle pe - cu - liar.
And so I

Bm
wake in the morn-ing and I step out - side, and I take a deep breath, and I get real high, and I

D
A
scream from the top of my lungs, "What's go - in' on?" And I say,

Chorus

A
Bm
"Hey, yeah, yeah, ay, ay. Hey, yeah, yay." I said, "Hey,

D
A
what's go - in' on?"
And I say,

Bm
"Hey, yeah, yeah, ay, ay.
Hey, yeah, yay."
I said, "Hey,

To Coda

D
A
what's go - in' on?"

Interlude

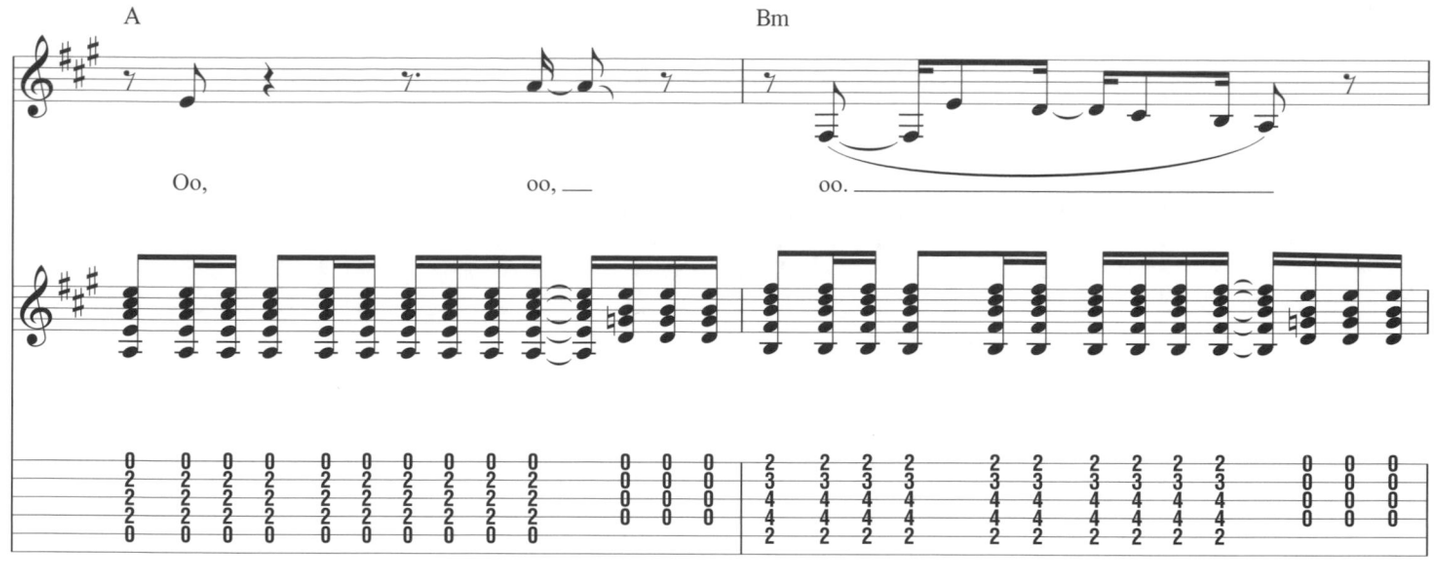

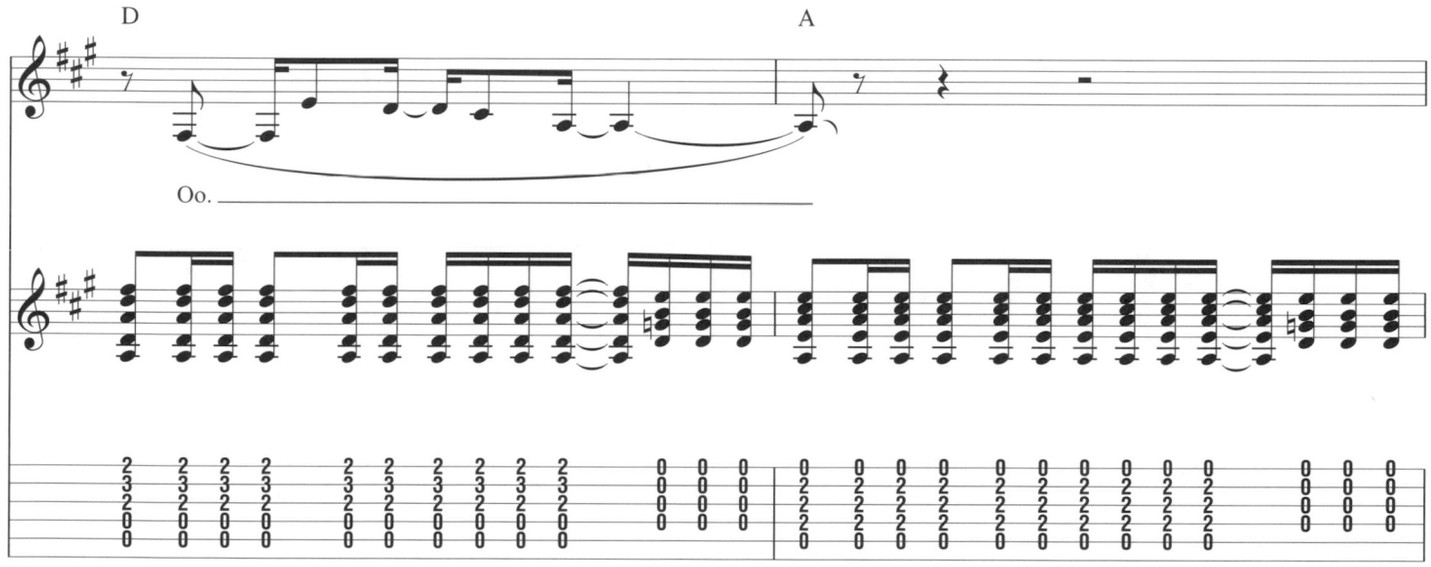

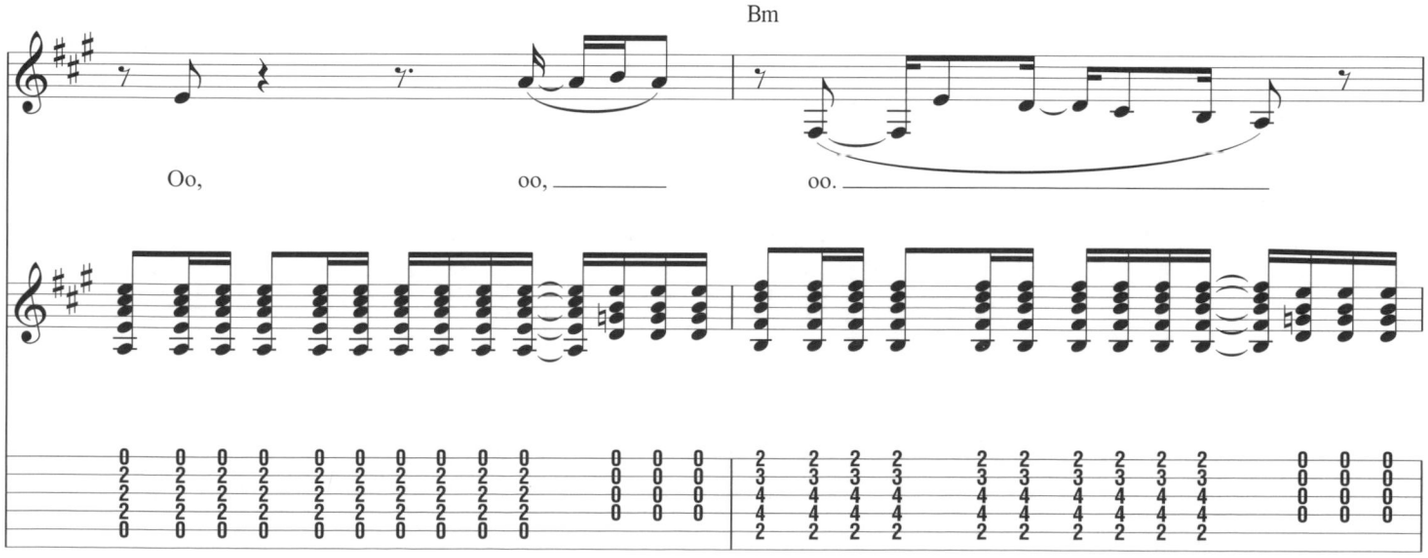

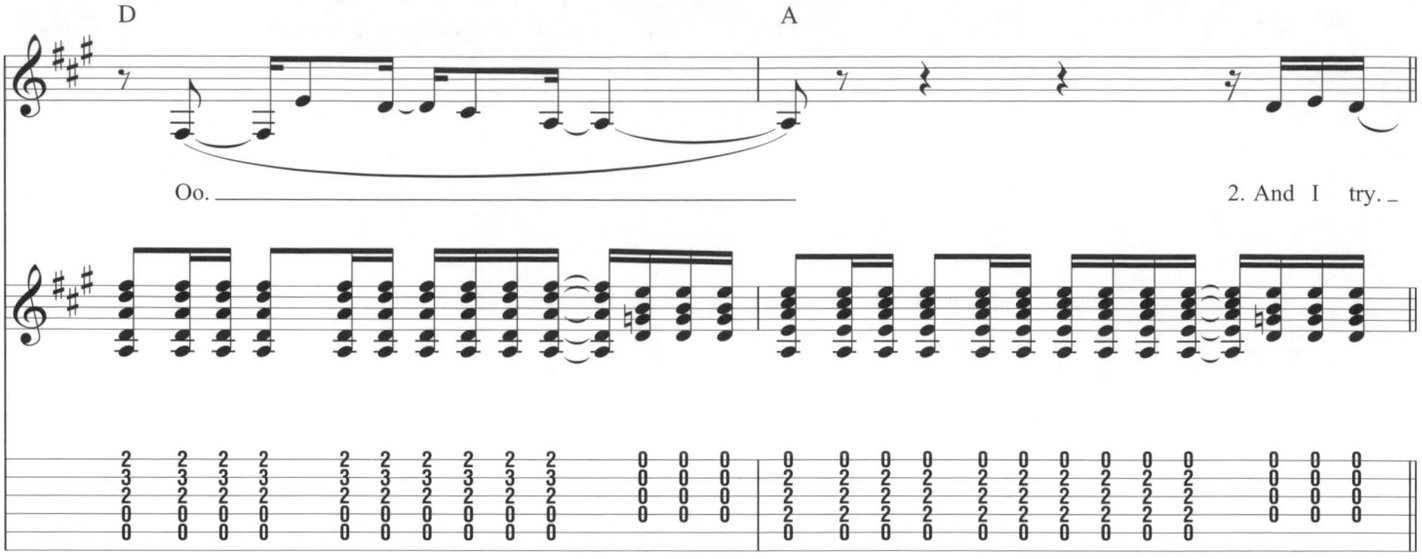
D
A
Oo.
2. And I try.

Verse

A
Bm
Oh my God, do I try.
I try all the time

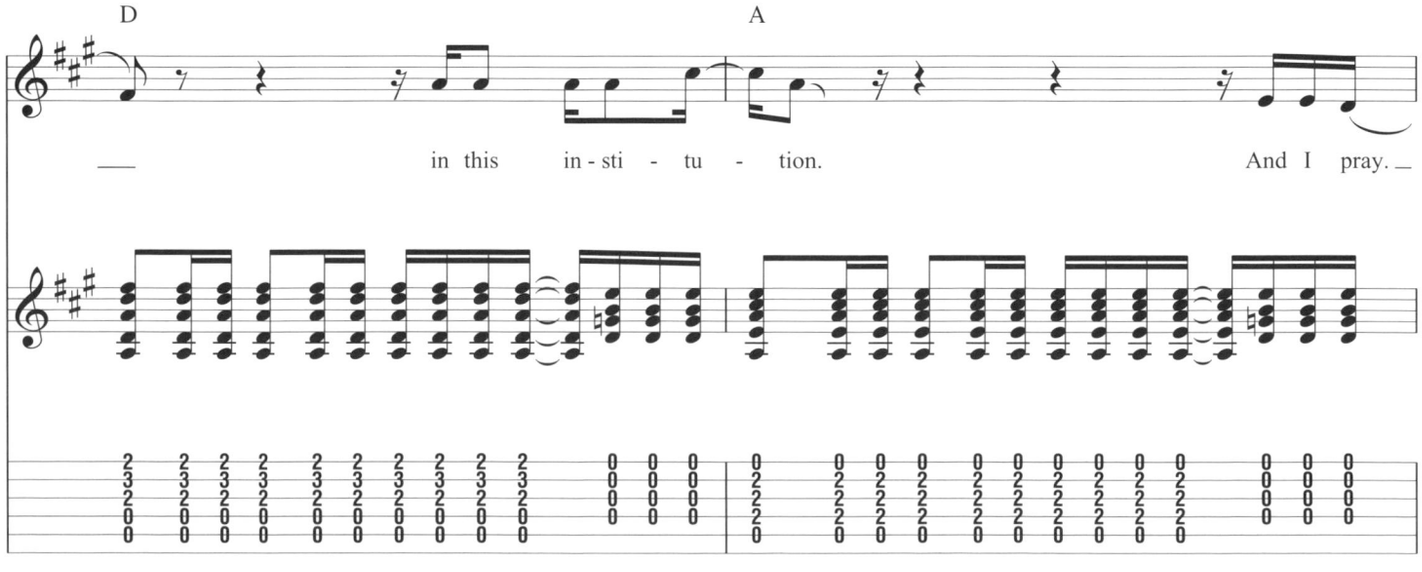
D
A
in this in - sti - tu - tion.
And I pray.

D.S. al Coda

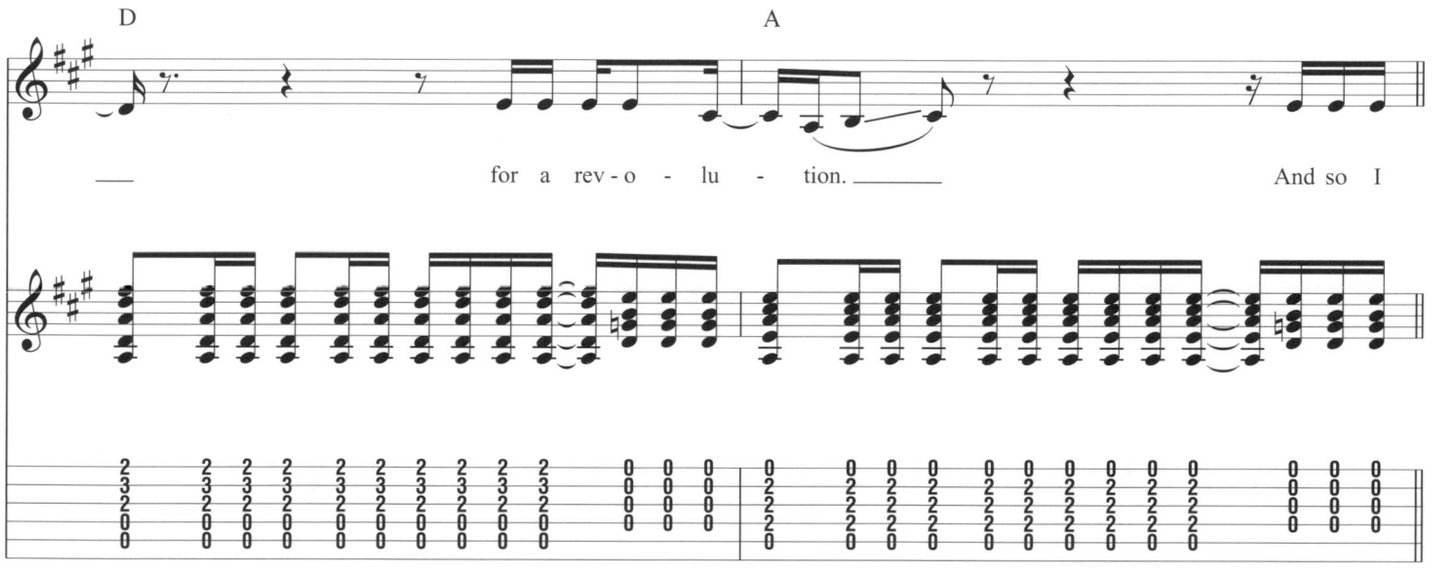

Coda

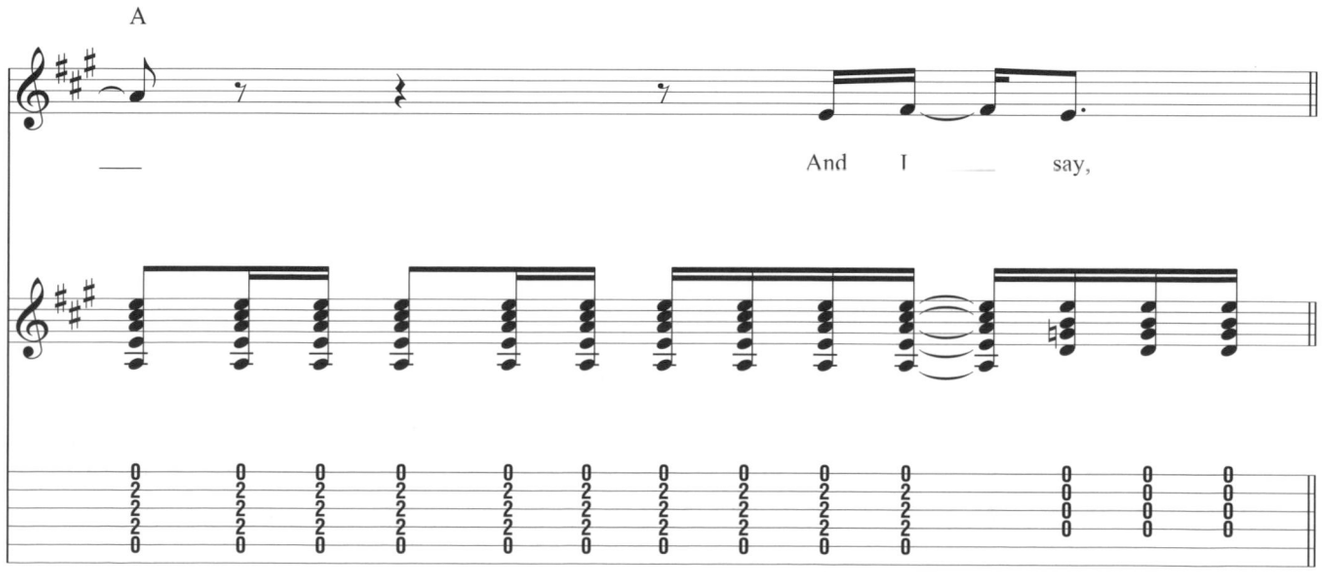

Bm
"Hey, yeah, yeah, ay, ay. Hey, yeah, yay." I said, "Hey,
(Wake up in the morn ing and I step out - side, take a deep breath and I get real high, and I

D
A
what's go - in' on?" And I say,
scream, "What's go - in' on?"

Outro

A
Bm
Oo, oo, oo.

Slower ♩= 57 (♫=♫)
D
A
Oo, uh - huh.
Bm
Twen - ty - five years and my life is still try'n' to get up that great big hill of hope
D
Dsus4
D Dsus2
A
rit.
for a des - ti - na - tion. Mm.
rit.

Redemption Song

Words and Music by Bob Marley

Copyright © 1980 Fifty-Six Hope Road Music Ltd. and Odnil Music Ltd.
All Rights in North America Administered by Blue Mountain Music Ltd./Irish Town Songs (ASCAP)
and throughout the rest of the world by Blue Mountain Music Ltd. (PRS)
All Rights Reserved

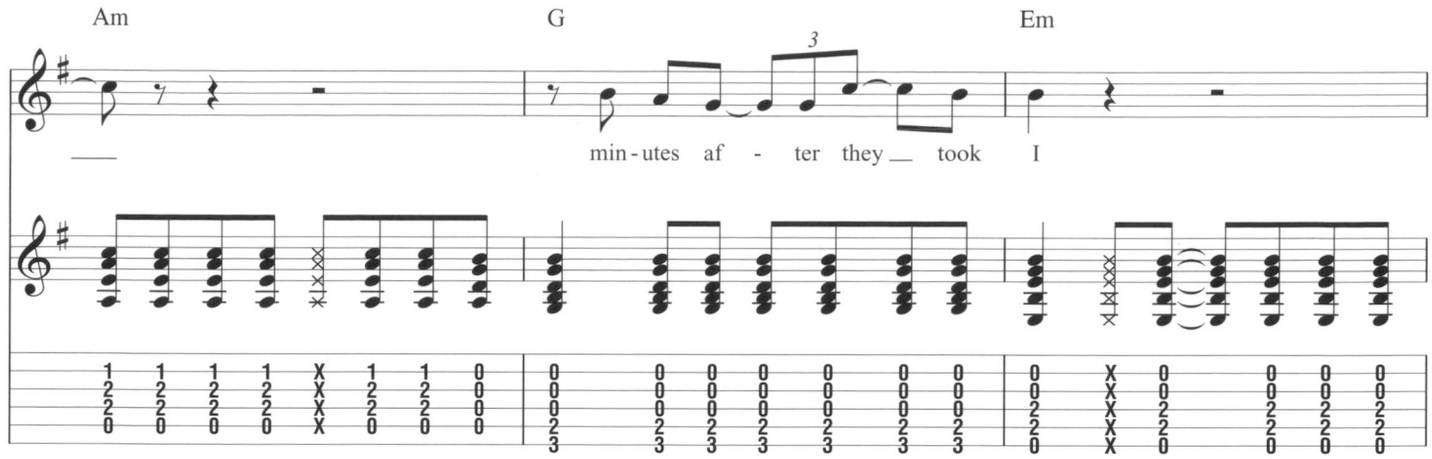
Am
G
Em
min - utes af - ter they took I

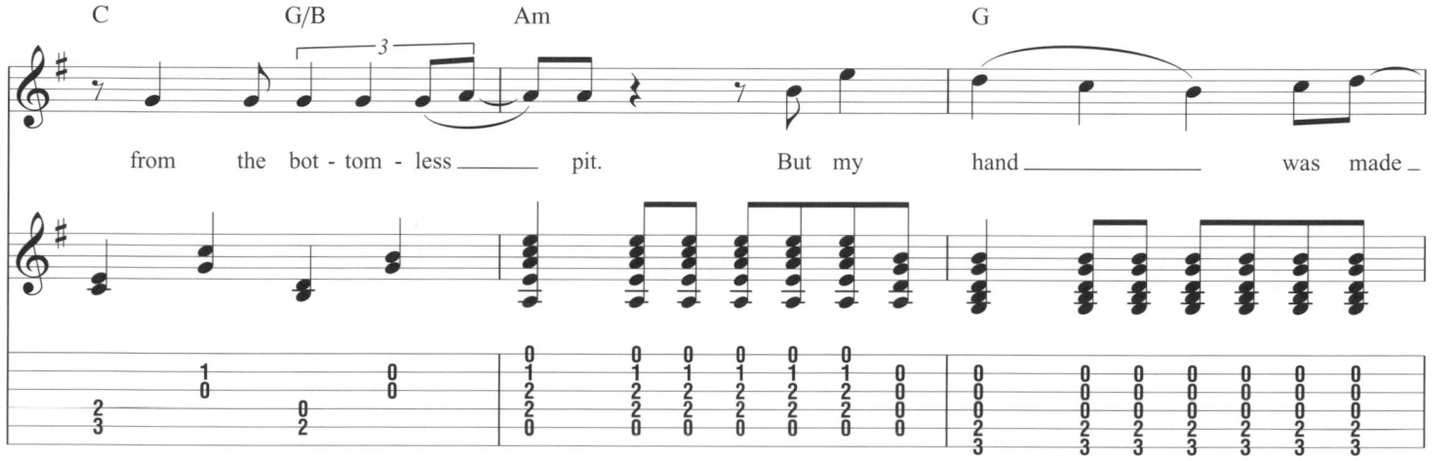
C
G/B
Am
G
from the bot - tom - less pit. But my hand was made

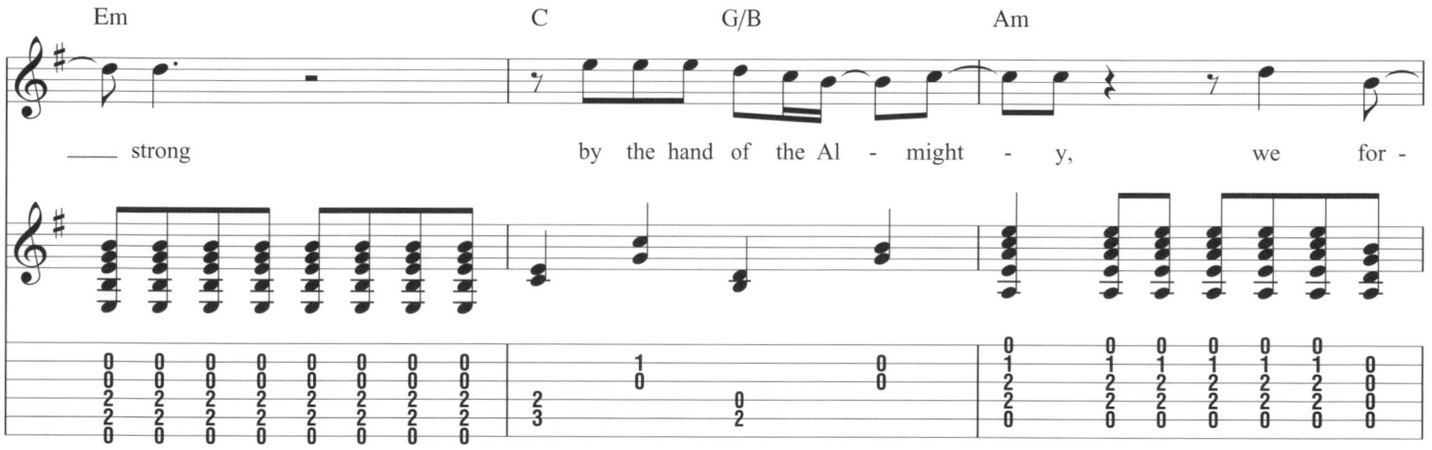
Em
C
G/B
Am
strong by the hand of the Al - might - y, we for -

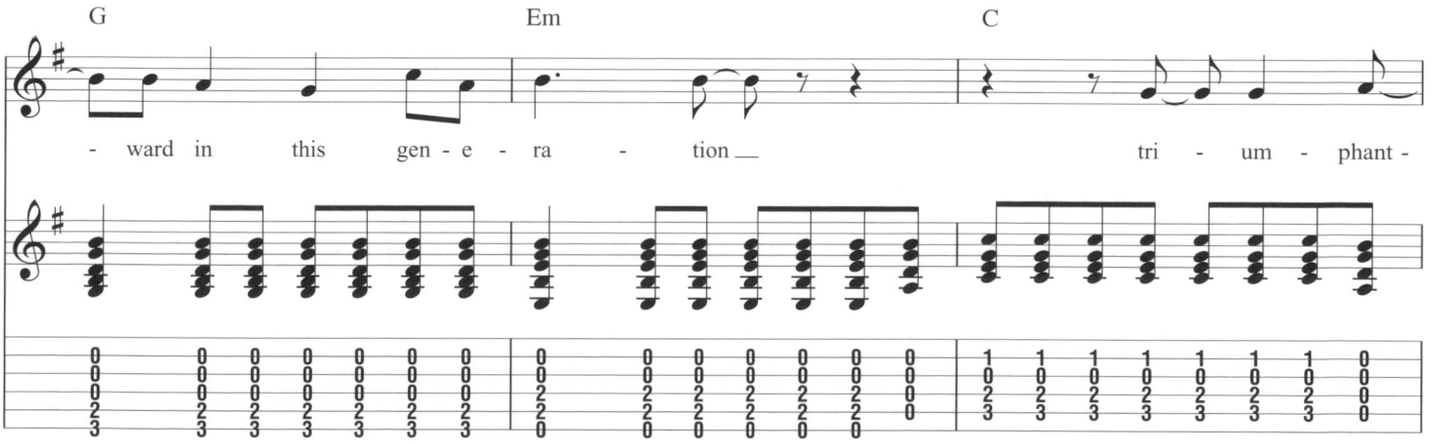
G
Em
C
- ward in this gen - e - ra - tion tri - um - phant -

Chorus
D5
G
- ly.
Won't you help to sing
C
D5
G
C
D5
these songs of free - dom?
'Cause all I ev - er have,
Em
C
D5
G
re - demp - tion songs,
C
D5
G
C
D5
re - demp - tion songs.
2. E - man - ci -

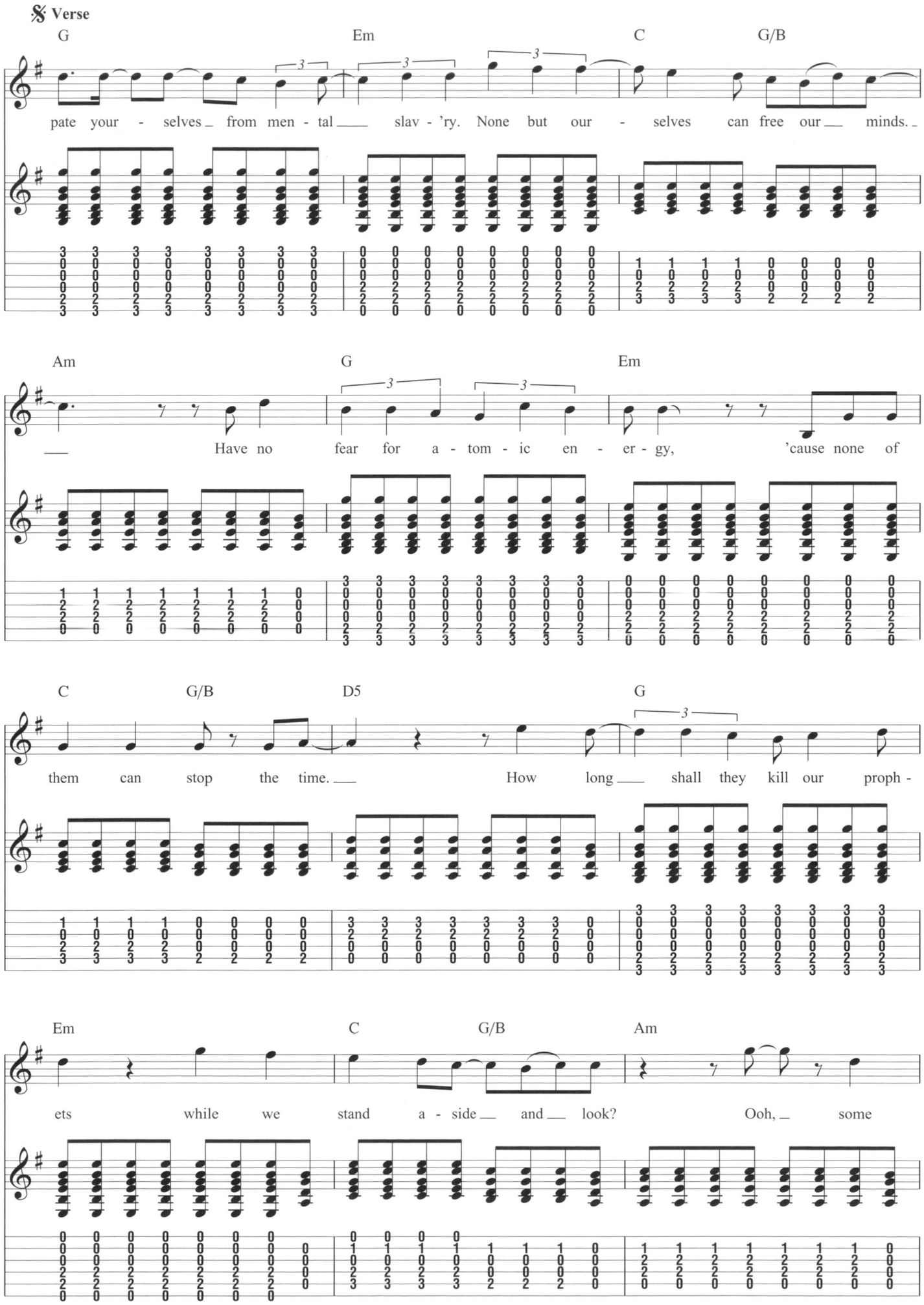
Verse
G Em C G/B
pate your - selves from men - tal slav - 'ry. None but our - selves can free our minds.
Am G Em
Have no fear for a - tom - ic en - er - gy, 'cause none of
C G/B D5 G
them can stop the time. How long shall they kill our proph -
Em C G/B Am
ets while we stand a - side and look? Ooh, some

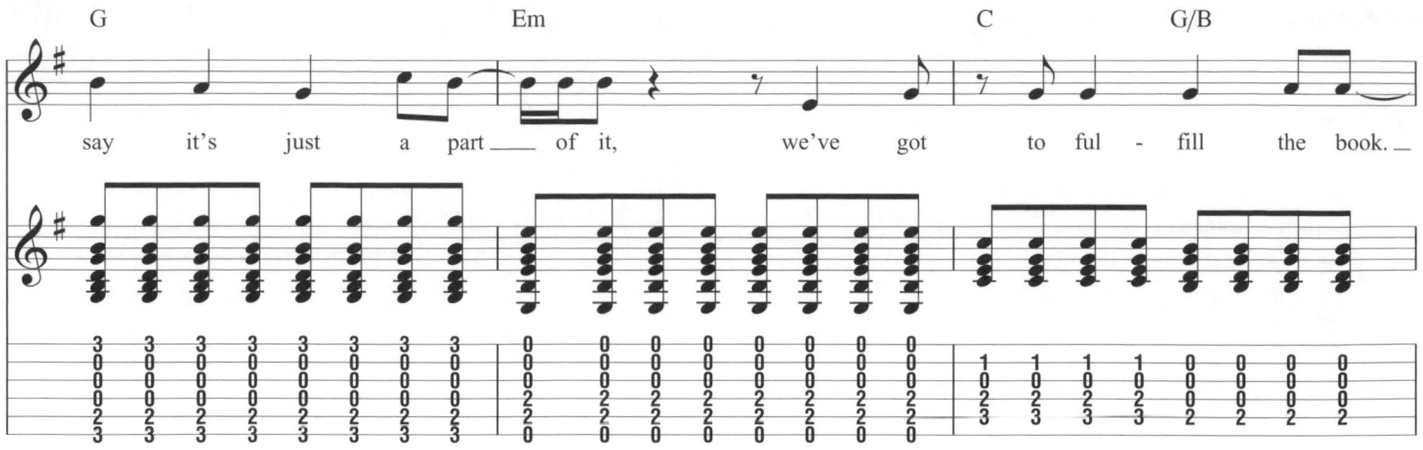
G
Em
C
G/B
say it's just a part of it, we've got to ful - fill the book.

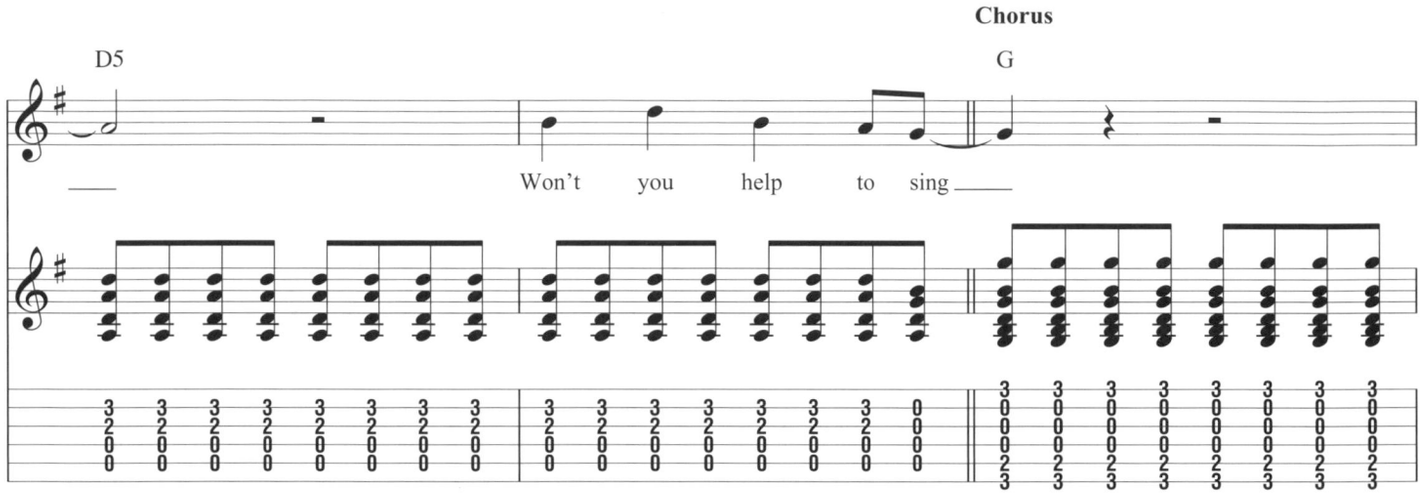
Chorus
D5
G
Won't you help to sing

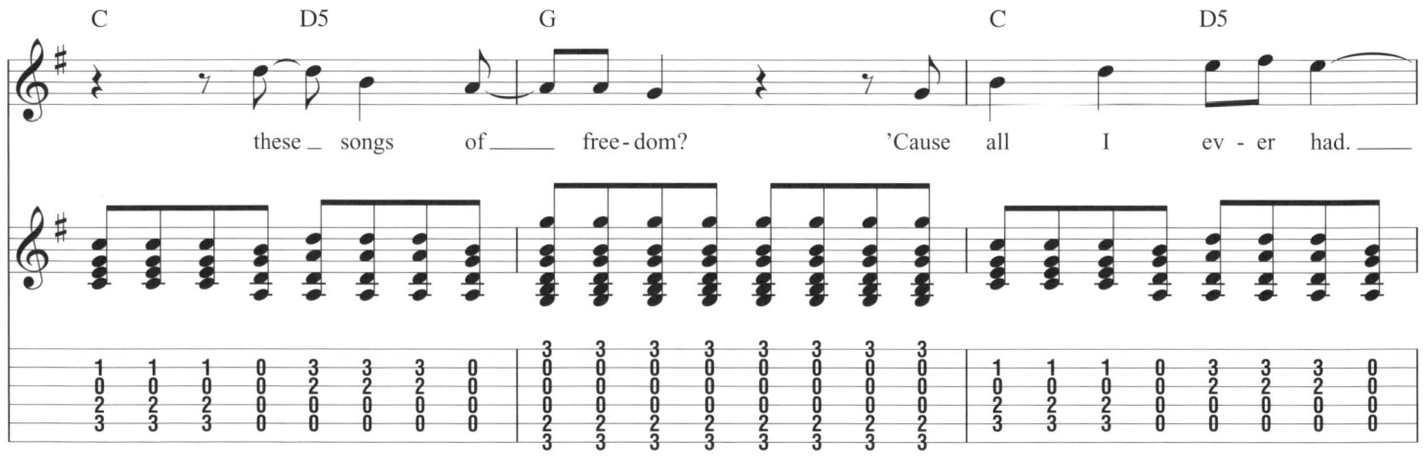
C
D5
G
C
D5
these songs of free-dom? 'Cause all I ev - er had.

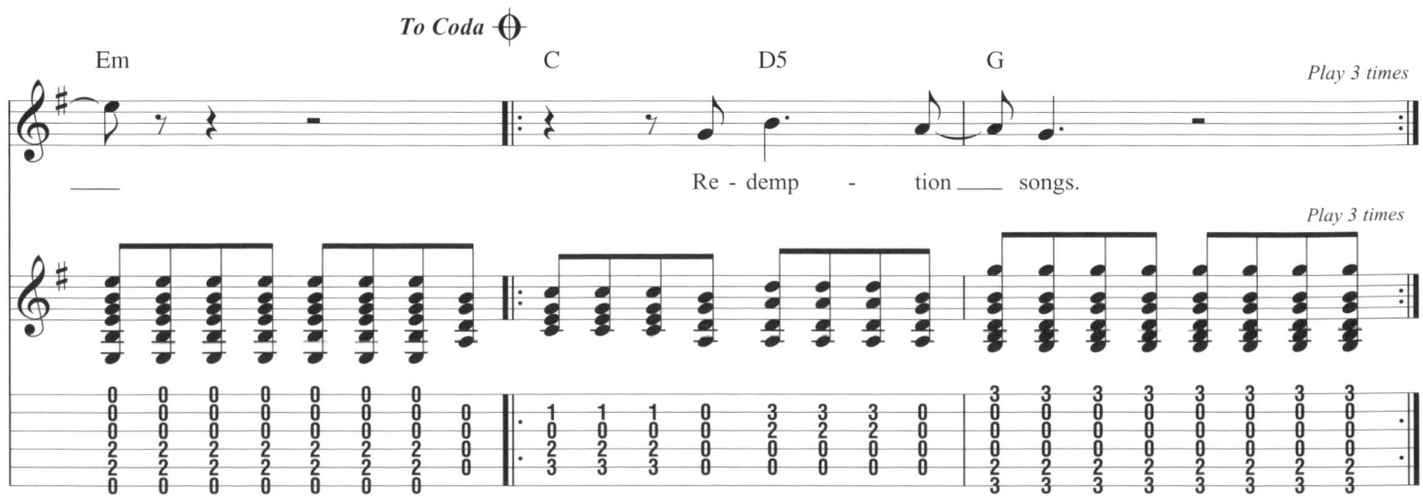
To Coda
Em
C
D5
G
Play 3 times
Re - demp - tion songs.
Play 3 times

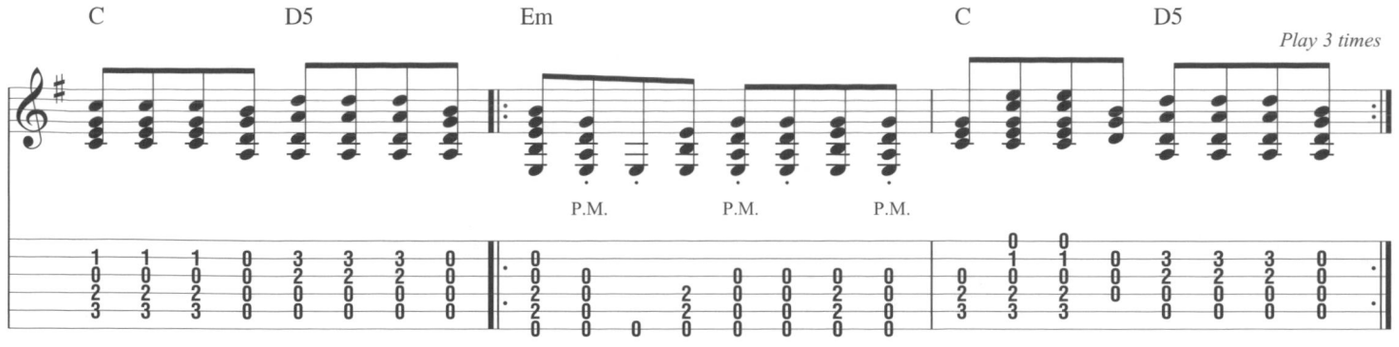
C
D5
Em
C
D5
Play 3 times
P.M.
P.M.
P.M.

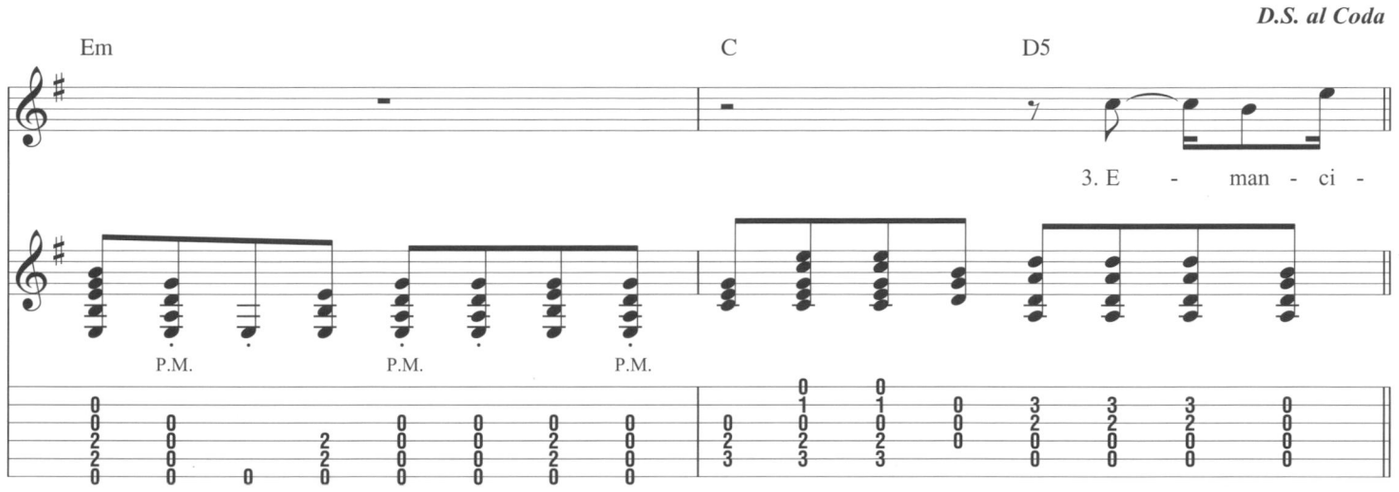
D.S. al Coda
Em
C
D5
3. E - man - ci -
P.M.
P.M.
P.M.

Coda
C
D5
G
C
D5
Re - demp - tion ___ songs,
all I ev - er had, ___

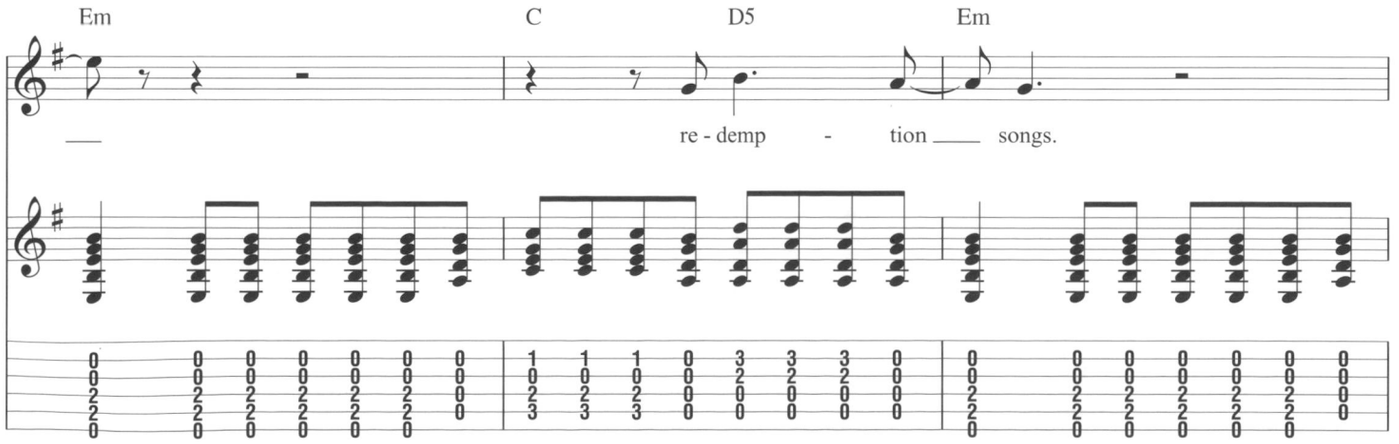
Em
C
D5
Em
___
re - demp - tion ___ songs.

C
D5
G
These songs of free - dom,

C
D5
G
songs of free - dom.

Outro

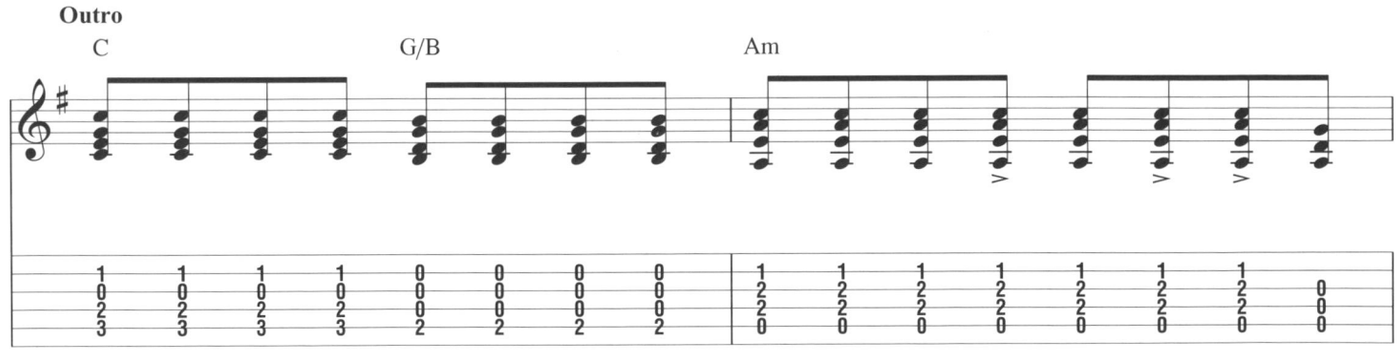
C
G/B
Am

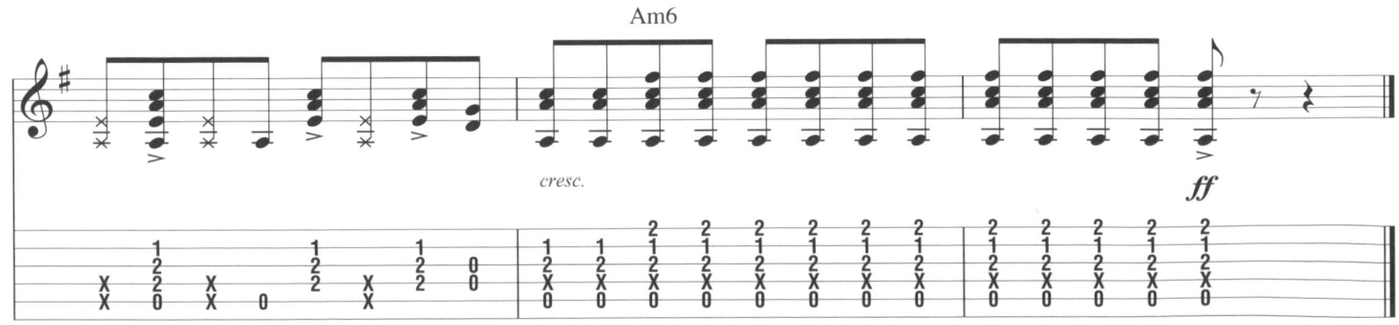
Am6
cresc.
ff